BizBest™
CONNECTIONS FOR SUCCESS

THE 100 BEST RESOURCES FOR SMALL BUSINESS

2004 EDITION

Daniel Kehrer

BizBest Media Corp.
Toll-free: 877-4-BizBest

www.BizBest.com
E-mail: info@BizBest.com

To Walker and Matt,
the two finest boys a Dad could have,
and to Kaye, whose patience and support
make the family strong.

Also from

BIZBEST™

BizBest: Connections for Success

Our flagship publication:
A ring-bound directory with over 2,000 small business
resources and exclusive BizBest analysis and ratings

BizBest by Daniel Kehrer

Nationally syndicated newspaper column

www.bizbest.com

Information and orders online

www.bizbest.org

Top-40 BizBest Q&A;
partnership with SCORE (www.score.org)

"Daniel Kehrer has condensed his expert knowledge on the small business marketplace into this superb book for entrepreneurs. BizBest delivers practical, objective resources for small business success."

— KEN YANCEY, CEO, SCORE Association

THE 100 BEST RESOURCES FOR SMALL BUSINESS

Daniel Kehrer

BizBest Media

Pacific Palisades

Publisher's Notes

BizBest Presents: **The 100 Best Resources for Small Business** is drawn from BizBest Media Corp's flagship publication, *BizBest: Connections for Success,* (ring-bound, annual) which lists nearly 2,000 resources and solutions for small business, with exclusive BizBest analysis and ratings. Suggested additions, corrections or comments are encouraged by e-mail to **editor@bizbest.com** or by regular mail to the address below.

Information published in **The 100 Best Resources for Small Business** is believed to be accurate and authoritative but is not intended to substitute for legal, accounting, tax or other professional advice. It is sold with the understanding that the publisher is not engaged in rendering professional business services. If expert assistance is required, the services of an appropriate professional should be sought. Statements and opinions expressed herein are not necessarily those of Biz Best Media or its affiliates.

ISBN 0-9719045-3-7 (paper)

Published by
BizBest Media Corporation
860 Via de la Paz, Suite D-4, Pacific Palisades, CA 90272
e-mail: info@bizbest.com • (310) 230-6868

© 2003 BizBest Media Corp.

Printed in the U.S.A.

10 9 8 7 6 5 4 3 2 1

WELCOME TO BIZBEST

Resources. Contacts. Solutions. These are today's most valuable assets for a small business. Business owners with access to the right connections will prosper. Delivering the best resources and solutions for the problems and opportunities you face is **BizBest's** sole mission. We continuously gather, rate and analyze thousands of potential resources in hundreds of subject areas vital to operating a small business, from accounting software, business plans and computers, to venture capital, Web services, zoning and everything in between.

Our flagship publication, *BizBest: Connections for Success*, describes in detail nearly 2,000 resources. *BizBest* has become a trusted companion of biz owners all across America because it does NOT accept advertising or paid listings of any kind. The proprietary analysis offered by our team of small business experts is 100% independent. We serve you, the business owner, not the corporate suits.

Now, for the first time, we've gathered **The 100 Best Resources for Small Business** in 12 key categories, including Startup, Sales & Marketing, Money & Finance, Management, Technology/Internet, Operations and Troubleshooting, and made this elite list, along with our analysis, easily available in paperback format.

BizBest Ratings

BizBest 100 resources serve small business in myriad ways. Some are household names; others you never heard of. The common bond is that they all offer some type of product, service, information or advice that is vital to business owners and startup entrepreneurs. No resource, of course, is perfect for every type of small business. In our ratings, however, we have tried to imagine what the best possible resource would look like to the broadest spectrum of small businesses looking for solutions in that area. A five-star rating is our best.

★★★★★ **Focus on Small Biz** — Does the resource/supplier focus specifically and expertly on the small business market?

★★★★★ **Easy Accessibility** — Is the product, service or information easy to access, and is the resource/supplier easy to deal with?

★★★★★ **Responsiveness** — Does the resource/supplier understand and respond to the specific needs of small business?

★★★★★ **Vital to Growth** — Are the solutions offered essential to helping your business grow and become more profitable?

★★★★★ **Value/Cost** — Does the resource/supplier provide exceptional value for any costs involved?

★★★★★ **Longevity** — Has the resource/supplier been in business for a significant amount of time and is it likely to have staying power?

Comments Welcome

I hope **BizBest** can help make your business an even bigger success. We welcome your comments. Send an e-mail to: editor@bizbest.com.

— **Daniel Kehrer, Founder & CEO, BizBest Media**

Contents

THE *100 BEST* BY SUBJECT CATEGORY

See page 9 for Alphabetical Index.

Contents — continued

Section 5: Operations

Section 6: Money & Finance

Section 7: Communications

Contents — continued

Section 8: Human Resources / Employees

Section 9: Government

Section 10: Import/Export

Section 11: Special Sectors (disabled, women, minorities, family, youth)

Section 12: Troubleshooting

THE BizBest® 100
Alphabetical Index
(page number adjacent to entry)

Startup

Business Plan Pro
(www.paloalto.com)

★★★★★ Focus on Small Biz
★★★★★ Easy Accessibility
★★★★ Responsiveness
★★ Vital to Growth
★★★★ Value/Cost
★★★★ Longevity
Best Feature: The Bplans.com Web site is a nice bonus.
Biggest Hangup: Can't actually write your plan for you.

Business Plan Pro, a feature-packed business plan software package from Palo Alto Software, will make writing your plan a snap. The 400 sample plans for different industries that come with it are extremely helpful. Answer yes or no to questions and the nifty *EasyPlan Wizard* selects the best outline, reports, charts and tables. Links to Web resources provide help with funding, research and plan distribution. Other resources help you access specialized data for more than 2,000 industries. There's even a library of templates to turn your plan into a slick computer presentation. Price is $99.95. A souped-up PREMIER version is $299. *Business Plan Toolkit Mac*, the Macintosh version, is $89.95 (download only). Even if you don't use the software, Palo Alto's Web site on creating business plans, called **Bplans.com (www.bplans.com)**, is a great place to find free startup tools and tips. Its real-life business plans and practical advice are the envy of the industry. Has a panel of experts who've answered 1,500 questions from entrepreneurs. This site can help you focus and define your business concept, compare industry ratios, set schedules, identify the types of people you will need and find funding. Search for sample plans on the site by type of business. Offers articles on getting your plan funded, buying a business, business plan legalities, making an e-commerce site successful and other topics. Sign up for the monthly *Planning Newsletter* with tips and advice. Tim Berry, the founder and CEO of Palo Alto Software who also contributes regularly to Bplans.com, really has it nailed.

BizBest ActionGuide: Business Plan Pro is available at major office and computer retailers, software discounters (for as little as $73) or direct from Palo Alto. Call **(888) PLAN-PRO**.

Small Business Owners Ask...

About Calculating Startup Costs

Dear BizBest: *I'm light on funds, trying to calculate the costs of starting a new business and want to be sure I'm not missing something big. Where can I get help (preferably free!)* — Starting Out

Dear Starting Out: Here's just the thing you need. **Bplans.com**, the business planning site from Palo Alto software, has a free **Starting Costs Calculator** that you can access online. It will help you determine how much money you'll need to start your business, using forecasts, analysis and "what-if" scenarios. You'll find it at **www.bplans.com/common/startcost**. Or look under TOOLS at Bplans.com. It's simple but helpful.

The Company Corporation
(www.corporate.com)

★★★★★ Focus on Small Biz
★★★★★ Easy Accessibility
★★★★ Responsiveness
★★ Vital to Growth
★★★★ Value/Cost
★★★★★ Longevity
Best Feature: 100+ years in biz, and you can incorporate online

This category leader has been providing incorporation and related biz services to entrepreneurs and small business owners since 1899. Talk about longevity! Through 25 affiliated offices, **The Company Corp.** helps business owners form some 125,000 new corporations yearly. Also handles limited liability companies (LLCs), registered agent services, corporate kits, publications and more. Not sure about which legal form to take? The Web site can help you compare options and make the right choice for your particular type of business. Get a free workbook or take a free online incorporation workshop. The Company Corp. is a time-tested place where you can get help choosing the right legal structure for your biz. Their online system is quick, reliable and easy to use. They also wrote **Incorporating Your Business For Dummies** (Hungry Minds, $21), which explains the incorporation process in as plain a terms as you will find anywhere. *Compliance Watch* is a tool that reduces record keeping and is free with the firm's registered agent service.

BizBest ActionGuide: You can incorporate online at the Web site or call **(800) 818-0204**; e-mail: info@corporate.com

FastTrac
(www.fasttrac.org)

★★★★★	Focus on Small Biz
★★★	Easy Accessibility
★★★	Responsiveness
★★	Vital to Growth
★★★★★	Value/Cost
★★	Longevity

Best Feature: Emphasizes hands-on, real-life training.
Biggest Hangup May not be available in your area.

FastTrac is an excellent and fast-growing educational program that operates nationwide, offering biz owners and entrepreneurs locally-based training programs and networking connections for a new or expanding enterprise. FastTrac is a creation of the **Ewing Marion Kauffman Foundation** (www.kauffman.org), a Kansas City-based non-profit that spends millions to promote entrepreneurship in America. The Kauffman Foundation also operates **Entreworld.org** (another *BizBest 100* resource), sponsors national entrepreneurship awards and supports entrepreneurship programs for kids (among other things). FastTrac conducts practical, hands-on business development programs and workshops, created and run by entrepreneurs. Offers hands-on training that helps entrepreneurs hone the skills needed to create, manage and grow a successful business. Here you don't just learn about business, you *live* it and work on your own venture throughout the course. FastTrac is offered in about 150 cities in 38 states through Chambers of Commerce, Small Business Development Centers, Women's Business Centers, Minority

Business Centers, universities, colleges, community colleges and individual consultants. For info on FastTrac in your area, and to sign up, go to "Where are FastTrac Programs Offered?" at the Web site and see if there is a FastTrac in your area. **This is a fabulous program** that lets you tap ideas and insights developed by hundreds of successful entrepreneurs. FastTrac has become one of America's top entrepreneurial training programs because it is written and taught *by* entrepreneurs, *for* entrepreneurs.

BizBest ActionGuide: See www.fasttrac.org for details and locations. Call **(800) 689-1740** or e-mail info@fasttrac.org

---

Small Business Owners Ask...
About Franchising

Dear BizBest: *My wife and I want to start our own business, and we are kicking around the idea of buying a franchise. Where can we can learn how franchising works and maybe find one that's right for us?* — Franchise Curious

Dear Curious: You're in good company. About 320,000 franchised small businesses in 75 industries now account for 40 percent of all U.S. retail sales. Franchise owners employ eight million people, a new franchise outlet opens every eight minutes and about one in every 12 retail businesses is part of a franchise. Here's our top resource.

International Franchise Assn.

★★★	Focus on Small Biz
★★★★	Easy Accessibility
★★★★	Responsiveness
★★	Vital to Growth
★★★★★	Value/Cost
★★★★	Longevity

Best Feature: Startup advice
Biggest Hangup Can be overly gung-ho on franchising

(www.franchise.org) The Washington, DC-based **International Franchise Assn.**, a membership group of franchisors, franchisees and suppliers, offers excellent info on franchise opportunities and development. Search their database of over 800 franchise companies with Web and e-mail links. Free help for beginners, with key questions to ask and info on home-based franchise opportunities. The Web site has a discussion forum and sections for minorities, women and veterans.

BizBest ActionGuide: At the site, click *Seeking a Franchise* to begin. Bookstore has helpful publications. Call **(202) 628-8000**; e-mail: ifa@franchise.org.

National Business Incubation Association
(www.nbia.org)

Based in Athens, OH, **NBIA** offers good basic info about business incubators and tips on selecting one. If you are considering an incubator or just want to learn more about how they work, NBIA can help. The group's greatest contribution to aspiring entrepreneurs is probably the Web site's "Links to Member Incubators" section which will help you find incubators in your area. Select your state and check out the offerings. Other information on the site is restricted to members and is only of interest to those operating business incubation centers.

★★★	Focus on Small Biz
★★★	Easy Accessibility
★★★	Responsiveness
★★	Vital to Growth
★★★★★	Value/Cost
★★★	Longevity

Best Feature: Incubator links
Biggest Hangup Most info for members only

BizBest ActionGuide: Visit the Web site or call **(740) 593-4331**; e-mail info@nbia.org.

SCORE
(www.score.org)

BizBest rates SCORE (Service Corps of Retired Executives) among the very top small biz resources in America, and one of the most under-appreciated. SCORE can provide you with your very own business consultant (usually a retired

★★★★★	Focus on Small Biz
★★★★	Easy Accessibility
★★★★	Responsiveness
★★★★	Vital to Growth
★★★★★	Value/Cost
★★★★★	Longevity

Best Feature: Expert advice, free
Biggest Hangup Should be better known nationwide

business exec) who will meet with you, face-to-face, to help you solve problems or answer questions on starting and growing your business. There are nearly 12,000 experienced SCORE counselors nationwide, and the service is **free and confidential.** Business counseling and workshops are offered at 389 SCORE chapter offices coast to coast. By meeting in person with a counselor, you get the advantage of local-market knowledge from a dedicated business volunteer. However, SCORE also offers free **e-mail counseling**, which has been a huge hit with business owners and startup entrepreneurs. About 800 counselors — with hundreds of specialties — are available online to answer questions and help you solve problems. Click on ASK SCORE at the Web site to search specialities and read bios of potential counselors to choose from. Questions can be submitted 24/7; answers generally follow within 48 hours. A key advantage is that you can select a counselor with specific expertise. There are over 600 unique skills in the databank. You will also find valuable advice and assistance in the Learning Center and Business Toolbox sections of the SCORE site — including some of the most popular BizBest Q&A columns on a special page. Also be sure to read some of the SCORE success stories posted on the Web site.

BizBest ActionGuide: To find an office near you call the national SCORE office in Washington, DC at **(800) 634-0245**. Or visit **www.score.org** and click on FIND SCORE to get the address, phone number and a map to your nearest office. Most SCORE chapters also have their own Web sites. See the list of links under FIND SCORE.

Small Business Development Centers
(www.sba.gov/sbdc)

SBDCs are another excellent and <u>free</u>, counseling and informational resource for small biz owners and startups. The U.S. Small Business Administration (SBA) administers this program, which offers a wide variety of info and guidance. There are small business development centers in every state, with a network of nearly 1,000 service locations at colleges, universities, vocational schools, chambers of commerce and economic development corporations nationwide. The SBDC

★★★★★	Focus on Small Biz
★★★★	Easy Accessibility
★★★★	Responsiveness
★★★★	Vital to Growth
★★★★★	Value/Cost
★★★★	Longevity
Best Feature: Wide range of help available for free	
Biggest Hangup Possible travel	

network delivers counseling, training and tech help in all aspects of small biz management, including financial, marketing, production, engineering and feasibility studies. Special programs include international trade, procurement assistance, finding venture capital and rural development. America's Small Business Development Center Network is the Federal Government's largest and most productive small business management and technical assistance program, serving 1.3 million small biz owners and aspiring entrepreneurs each year.

BizBest ActionGuide: For locations, click on YOUR NEAREST SBDC at **www.sba.gov/sbdc**. You can also visit the **Association of Small Business Development Centers** Web site (**www.asbdc-us.org**) to find locations (click on LOCAL SERVICES). Call ASBDC at: **(703) 764-9850**; e-mail: info@asbdc-us.org. For Business Information Center (BIC) locations go to **www.sba.gov/BI/bics/** or call **800-8-ASK-SBA**.

SBA **Business Information Centers** are a related program, offering self-help computer hardware and software, plus a library to help you plan a new biz or expand an existing one. Use BIC resources as often as you wish for *free*. More than 80 BICs are operating in these locations: Jonesboro and Pine Bluff AR; Los Angeles, San Diego, Chula Vista, San Francisco and San Jose CA; Denver CO; Hartford CT; Wilmington DE; Washington DC; Jacksonville FL; Atlanta GA; Honolulu, HI; Boise ID; Chicago IL; Indianapolis IN; Keokuk and Waterloo, IA; Louisville KY; Lewiston, Portland and Springvale ME; Baltimore and Cumberland, MD; Boston, Cape Cod, Lawrence, Lynn, Pittsfield, Worcester, Brockton, West Barnstable and Lawrence MA; Flint and Grand Rapids MI; Minneapolis MN; Kansas City MO; Helena, Billings and Bozeman MT; Omaha NE; Las Vegas NV; Nashua, Keene, Bethlehem, Laconia, Springvale and Conway NH; Newark and Camden NJ; Albuquerque NM; Albany NY; Grand Forks and Minot ND; Cleveland OH; Oklahoma City OK; Warm Springs, Grand Ronde, Chiloquin and Portland OR; Pittsburgh PA; Santurce PR; Providence RI; Charleston SC; Rapid City, Sioux Falls and Yankton SD; Nashville, Memphis and Jackson TN; El Paso, Ft. Worth and Houston TX; Salt Lake City and Ogden UT; Burlington VT; Manassas and Richmond VA; Seattle, Spokane, Richland, Auburn and Mt. Vernon WA; Fairmont WV; Casper WY. To see if a BIC will be opening in your area, call **(202) 205-6665**.

StartupJournal.com
(www.startupjournal.com)

Startup Journal — *THE WALL STREET JOURNAL Center for Entrepreneurs* — offers guidance on starting or buying a business or franchise, with business planning tools and lists of franchise opportunities, businesses for sale and venture capital firms, plus articles from *The Wall Street Journal*. The feature stories, new each day on the home page, are worth a regular visit. Startup Journal carries lots of how-to information and with the muscle of the Dow Jones media empire behind it, the reporting is always solid, reliable and entertaining. Startup Journal's sections — Columnists, How-To, Ideas, Franchising, Financing,

★★★★★	Focus on Small Biz
★★★★	Easy Accessibility
★★★★	Responsiveness
★★★	Vital to Growth
★★★	Value/Cost
★★★	Longevity

Best Feature: Daily updates and WSJ connection
Biggest Hangup: Sponsorships sometimes get in the way

Technology and Running a Business — carry practical advice and real-world examples. Online search and tool functions that help you build a business plan (Palo Alto Software), or find trade shows (TSNN), businesses for sale (BizBuySell), trademarks (NameProtect) and business lawyers (Lawyers.com) are all run by the respective outside services.

BizBest ActionGuide: You'll get the most out of this by reading the features and columnists, as business reporting is what they do best.

Small Business Owners Ask...
About Finding a Business Lawyer

Dear BizBest: *I need legal help on a specialized venture capital matter. How do I connect with knowledgeable business lawyers?* — Need Law

Dear Law: StartupJournal.com's *Business Legal Center* has a free "Find a Lawyer" service (through Martindale-Hubbell Lawyers.com). Search by location and dozens of business specialties — including venture capital. There's also great legal info on starting a biz and tips for finding a lawyer. Look in the HOW-TO section, on the right side.

Management & Training

BizBest® 100

bCentral
(www.bcentral.com)

This well-organized and helpful service from Microsoft Corp., calls itself "The world's #1 site for small business." While that's debatable, Bill Gates certainly has the money muscle to put up a great site. **bCentral** is all about helping biz owners manage everyday processes and is packed with useful services and info. Whether you want to build a successful Web presence, boost your marketing, sales and

★★★★★	Focus on Small Biz
★★★★	Easy Accessibility
★★	Responsiveness
★★★	Vital to Growth
★★★	Value/Cost
★★★★	Longevity

Best Feature: Ability to integrate with other Microsoft solutions
Biggest Hangup Its Microsoft

service, or manage operations, bCentral has solutions to meet your needs. And since this is Microsoft, many products and services are integrated with tools you already know, like *Microsoft Office.* Most bCentral solutions are available for a free 30-day test-drive. You'll also find practical tips, news, advice, how-to articles and much more. Products/services include: Web hosting and e-mail ■ appointment scheduling ■ e-commerce management ■ e-mail marketing and list building ■ sales leads ■ marketing tools ■ Web collaboration ■ Retail management and business listings ■ search engine submission, and others. *Microsoft Small Business Manager,* available through bCentral, is a sophisticated software suite for small companies that have outgrown standalone software solutions. *Manager* integrates financial management, sales, purchasing, inventory, payroll and other functions into a single software package that costs $995.

BizBest ActionGuide: bCentral's home page is mostly advertising for Microsoft services. Select NEWS & RESOURCES at the top for helpful advice on finance, human resources, legal and other topics. Call **(866) 223-6872** for product info.

Business Owner's Toolkit
(www.toolkit.cch.com)

A creation of **CCH Inc.**, this multi-talented small business resource calls itself *"Total know-how for small business."* That may overstate it — but only a little. *Business Owner's Toolkit brims with practical advice and info.* Using the site is free, but CCH wants to sell you its products/services along the way (that's okay, since they are generally great). CCH is a highly-respected outfit, and you can count on their information being thoroughly-researched, authoritative and timely. Toolkit includes the following: ■ **CCH Small Business Guide**: Thousands of pages of information vital to running and growing a small business; ■ **Business Tools**: Downloadable checklists, model biz plans, forms and other documents; ■ **HR Tools**: Interactive employment tools and coursework; ■ **Ask Alice!**: Their online advice columnist; ■ **CCH Online Store**: Books on small business topics; and ■ **E-mail**

★★★★★ Focus on Small Biz
★★★★ Easy Accessibility
★★★★ Responsiveness
★★★★ Vital to Growth
★★★★★ Value/Cost
★★★★★ Longevity
Best Feature: Authoritative beyond comparison
Biggest Hangup: Finding your way among all that's offered

Newsletter: Monthly updates on developments affecting small business. The **Health Care Benefits** section has an excellent overview of health insurance for small business owners. Covers pros and cons of offering health insurance; which benefits you should offer; how to find and choose benefit providers; how to negotiate health plan contracts and what paperwork you'll face. The **SOHO Guidebook** has thousands of pages of info on starting, financing, managing and marketing a small biz.

BizBest ActionGuide: General inquiries call **(800) 835-5224**.

ALSO OF INTEREST FROM CCH: A CCH division called **KnowledgePoint** (**www.knowledgepoint.com**) is a top publisher of employee management software (*People Manager, Ultimate Employer*) and creator of **HRTools.com**, a Web-based virtual HR department. With HRTools you can create a personnel policy manual, determine if you are correctly classifying workers as independent contractors, subscribe to a performance appraisal system, get info on how to properly fire someone, and more. Call **KnowledgePoint** at **(800) 727-1133**.
Complete Tax (**www.completetax.com**) is CCH's online tax return service. Call **(800) 248-3248**.

★★★	Focus on Small Biz
★★★★	Easy Accessibility
★★★	Responsiveness
★★★	Vital to Growth
★★★	Value/Cost
★★★	Longevity
Best Feature: Broad selection	
Biggest Hangup Knowing exactly what you're getting	

Digital 2000
(**www.trainingprofessionals.com**)
Need training materials for your biz? This boutique site is the place! **Digital 2000** produces affordable safety training videos, DVDs and CD-ROMs for small biz, and has been doing this gig since about 1985. Hundreds of available topics cover everything from ladders, hand tools and heavy equipment, to online safety, chemicals and almost any occupation you can think of. Check the index at the Web site for an A to Z list. Most are $69 to $99. This is a BizBest 100 member that does one thing, and does it well. Period.

BizBest ActionGuide: Visit the Web site; call **(800) 334-1523**; or e-mail: products@digital-2000.com.

Edward Lowe Foundation
(www.edwardlowe.org)

★★★	Focus on Small Biz
★★★★	Easy Accessibility
★★★	Responsiveness
★★★	Vital to Growth
★★★★	Value/Cost
★★	Longevity

Best Feature: Fills niche for 2nd stage biz owners
Biggest Hangup: Still new and not well known

Bankrolled by the originator of Kitty Litter (Edward Lowe, who died in 1995), the **Edward Lowe Foundation** champions the entrepreneurial spirit of *"second stage"* and emerging growth business owners by helping support and foster networking opportunities for those individuals. A second-stage business is considered past startup, but not yet professionally managed, and typically has between $1 million and $50 million in sales. This is a small biz niche that has needed some beefing up, and the Lowe folks are doing a bang-up job. The Foundation's term for what it provides is *PeerSpectives*, and they've developed a wonderful newsletter and Web site (**www.peerspectives.org**) for the *PeerSpectives* brand. This is a top resource for established, growth-stage biz owners looking to network with peers and find the best ideas for *growth* (rather than survival), plus insight and inspiration from other owners. Subscribe to the monthly *PeerSpectives* newsletter and Web site, and find state-by-state links to biz owner peer groups at the main Foundation site. The PeepSpectives brand is still rather new, and longevity is unproven.

BizBest ActionGuide: HQ: somewhere near Cassopolis, MI; call **(800) 232-5693**; e-mail: info@lowe.org.

Entrepreneur.com

Entrepreneur.com — kin to the *Entrepreneur* magazine group — is one of the most-visited Web sites serving small business. Offers tons of practical information and articles, expert answers from business consultants and a wide range of services designed to solve challenges entrepreneurs face daily. Sections include: Start-ups, Home Biz, Franchise, Money, Marketing, Management, e-Biz, Tech and The Magazine. The vast storehouse of magazine material offers excellent and

★★★★★	Focus on Small Biz
★★★★	Easy Accessibility
★★★	Responsiveness
★★★	Vital to Growth
★★★★	Value/Cost
★★★★	Longevity

Best Feature: Great info on the basics & franchising
Biggest Hangup: Ads pay their bills, but get intrusive at times

comprehensive help for starting, running or growing a successful business. As just one example, **Entrepreneur Magazine's FormNet** is a terrific place to download ready-to-use *MSWord*-compatible forms for biz purposes such as: Analysis, Collection/Credit, Financial Management, Human Resources, Inventory, Leasing, Legal, Market Research, Memos and Sales. Quickest way there: go to **www.entrepreneur.com** and search for FormNet at the home page. Entrepreneur.com is so extensive that you can return time after time and keep finding new things.

BizBest ActionGuide: Explore the site. Entrepreneur has always been strong in the franchising field and the Franchise Zone is extensive.

EntreWorld
(**www.entreworld.org**)

★★★★★	Focus on Small Biz
★★★★★	Easy Accessibility
★★★	Responsiveness
★★★★	Vital to Growth
★★★★★	Value/Cost
★★★★	Longevity

Best Feature: Non-profit so there are no ads

Biggest Hangup: Approach is somewhat academic at times

The Kauffman Foundation operates **EntreWorld** (www.entreworld.org), which is without a doubt one of the most extensive and useful small biz Web sites yet created. *These folks are highly dedicated, well funded and really know what they're doing.* It's all free and carries no advertising. **EntreWorld** has no agenda other than to further the growth and understanding of entrepreneurship in America. EntreWorld divides itself into three worlds: 1) Starting a business; 2) Growing an existing business; and 3) Academic materials to support entrepreneurship education. All three sections are strong and are supported by the Web site's exclusive **Entrepreneur's Search Engine**, which can help you find just the information you're looking for. Sections are neatly divided into topics, such as Finance, Marketing & Sales, Technology and others, making it easy to navigate. If business or tech terminology is hanging you up, EntreWorld's excellent GLOSSARY has all the answers you need. There's also a link to **Small-Business-Dictionary.org**, a helpful reference site explaining some 2,500 startup and small business topics, terms and phrases.

BizBest ActionGuide: The Kauffman Foundation is based in Kansas City, MO; call **(888) 777-GROW**; e-mail: info@entreworld.org.

National Association for the Self-Employed
(www.nase.org)

NASE champions the self-employed and owners of "micro-businesses" (under 10 employees), who are mostly home-based. Membership gets you access to business tools, tips and training, plus discounts on services such as legal advice, payroll, health insurance and many others. NASE began in 1981 mainly as

★★★★★	Focus on Small Biz
★★★★	Easy Accessibility
★★★	Responsiveness
★★	Vital to Growth
★★★★	Value/Cost
★★★	Longevity

Best Feature: Group insurance
Biggest Hangup: Selling you too-much insurance

a means of selling group insurance to the self-employed. Now the group has about 200,000 members and offers tools and resources for the self-employed, along with political representation and insurance benefits.

BizBest ActionGuide: Basic dues are $96/year. See the full benefits lineup at the Web site or call **(800) 232-6273.**

National Federation of Independent Business
(www.nfib.com)

NFIB — the largest (600,000 strong) and one of the oldest small biz organizations in America — is one membership every small business owner should have. This grass roots group offers small biz owners nationwide the best means available of getting involved in the political decision-making process that shapes small business policy at local,

★★★★★	Focus on Small Biz
★★★★★	Easy Accessibility
★★★★★	Responsiveness
★★★★★	Vital to Growth
★★★★★	Value/Cost
★★★★★	Longevity

Best Feature: Members have a vote on all positions
Biggest Hangup: Takes itself very seriously

state and federal levels. *NFIB is considered the single most influential business lobbying group in Washington, DC.* And beyond that, the NFIB provides its members access to discounts on dozens of key products and services — as much as 60% on shipping (FedEx and Roadway), computer hardware and software (Gateway; QuickBooks), Internet and Web site services

(Website Pros/IBM), business insurance (The Hartford), merchant services (Solveras Payment Systems), payroll services (Paymaxx), travel and others. After shunning member services in favor of pure politics for most of its first 50 years (the group began in 1943), NFIB's lineup of benefits and perks has grown longer and more impressive in recent years. Click on "Member Benefits" at **NFIB.com** for a complete catalog of offerings. Members receive *MyBusiness*, a well-executed bi-monthly magazine full of helpful information on operating a successful business (*BizBest* CEO Daniel Kehrer was founding editor of this magazine in 1989, when it was called *Independent Business*). And because NFIB is active in all 50 states, you'll also be kept abreast of key small business issues in your state. Dues are reasonable — join online for a year for a single payment of $200, or pay $20 a month. The NFIB Web site is also a treasure trove of helpful small biz info and advice — *some of it available to non-members as well*. The Business Toolbox section, for example, lets you search an extensive database of small biz topics and solutions, from accounting and insurance, to legal issues, shipping, staffing and more. You can tap advice from peers and get the inside scoop from Washington and all 50 state capitals. NFIB membership is vital for any biz owner who wants to be truly plugged into the small business community.

BizBest ActionGuide: Visit **www.nfib.com** or call **(800) NFIB-NOW.**

Nolo Press
(www.nolo.com)

★★★★	Focus on Small Biz
★★★	Easy Accessibility
★★★★	Responsiveness
★★	Vital to Growth
★★★★	Value/Cost
★★★★	Longevity

Best Feature: Talks plain English
Biggest Hangup: You need time to read it all

Nolo Press, a publisher of self-help legal aids, has an absolute knack for knowing the types of information small biz owners need most. Nolo's list of specialized products for small business is lengthy, covering just about any topic you can think of. Their affordable, jargon-free books, software, legal forms and Web resources are also available in versions you can download. And their Web site is a dream (well, as much as anything involving legal stuff can be). Browse the free *Small Business Law Center* (click "Small Business" under Law Centers) for concise, plain English info. The site answers questions about patents, trademarks and copyrights, too.

BizBest ActionGuide: Find Nolo titles in the business or self-help legal section of book stores. The Nolo Web site has complete info, or call **(800) 992-6656.**

★★★★★	Focus on Small Biz
★★★	Easy Accessibility
★★★	Responsiveness
★★	Vital to Growth
★★★★	Value/Cost
★★★	Longevity

Best Feature: Jane's touch
Biggest Hangup: Not enough

SBTV.com

SBTV (Small Business TV) is a Web-based network that carries information and advice of interest to business owners and entrepreneurs. SBTV experts help solve small biz problems of all kinds. This is an invention of **Jane Applegate**, the author of several popular small biz books, including *The Entrepreneur's Desk Reference* (2003). SBTV offers "channels" on protecting your business, women biz owners, small biz profiles, employee (HR) management, business finance and more.

BizBest ActionGuide: Visit the site.

Service Quality Institute
(www.customer-service.com)

Minneapolis-based **Service Quality Institute** is headquarters for customer service solutions. Although it does not specifically target small business, most of the information applies to small companies as well as large. John Tschohl (pronounced Schole), who formed Service Quality Institute in 1972, is a fanatic about customer service and was one of the leaders in the field well before it became "hot" in the 1980s and 90s. Says Tschohl, "Do less than customers expect and service is perceived as bad. Do exactly what customers expect and service is perceived as good. But do more than customers expect and service is perceived as superior." The Institute can help you keep customers by developing a culture of superior customer service. Offers 30 customer service training programs. Sign up for the free Strategic Customer Service newsletter.

★★★	Focus on Small Biz
★★★	Easy Accessibility
★★★★	Responsiveness
★★	Vital to Growth
★★★★	Value/Cost
★★★★	Longevity

Best Feature: Top expertise
Biggest Hangup: Talks to bigger companies, too

BizBest ActionGuide: Visit the Web site; call **(952) 884-3311**; or e-mail: quality@servicequality.com.

Small Business Advocate
(www.smallbusinessadvocate.com)

Jim Blasingame — a.k.a. **The Small Business Advocate** — is one of the best friends small business has ever had. His radio show on Talk America Radio Network is an inspiration. Every weekday morning he and his Brain Trust members discuss issues and opportunities of small biz ownership, with tips on how to be more successful. What makes it so great is the *real-world perspective* that Blasingame brings to the table. The small biz community he's built around the show and his Web site is a place where entrepreneurs can find ideas, answers and encouragement. The Small Business Advocate Web site offers hundreds of free resources arranged in "Small Business Suites" such as

★★★★★	Focus on Small Biz
★★★	Easy Accessibility
★★★★	Responsiveness
★★★	Vital to Growth
★★★★	Value/Cost
★★★	Longevity

Best Feature: Brain Trust
Biggest Hangup: Finding them on the radio

Management Fundamentals, Marketing, Advertising & Branding, Small Business Technology, Home-based & Teleworking, Inspirational/Motivational and Women in the Marketplace. There's nothing to join. Just show up at the Web site or tune in the show and you're a "member." The Web site carries a live Internet simulcast of the talk show, a daily replay feature and a searchable audio archives, plus hundreds of print articles. **It's all free and dedicated to your success.** Be sure to sign up for Jim's timely and informative e-newsletter (also free). If you could bring just one guy along in your small biz lifeboat, Jim's the person you'd want.

BizBest ActionGuide: Visit the site. Call **(888) 823-2366**; e-mail dsd@jbsba.com.

Section **3**

Technology and the Internet

Ask Dr. Tech
(**www.askdrtech.com**)

Tech support from computer hardware and software makers or service providers can be crummy. Just finding a phone number is a challenge. Many companies deliberately discourage support calls. Then you wait — 5, 10, 20 minutes and up. If your problem involves multiple software, hardware or service brands, the rep may point a finger elsewhere. Then you start again. Some manufacturers even charge a fee.

★★☆	Focus on Small Biz
★★★★	Easy Accessibility
★★★	Responsiveness
★★★★★	Vital to Growth
★★★★	Value/Cost
★★	Longevity
Best Feature: 24/7 support	
Biggest Hangup: The cost	

Now there's a better way to keep all your tech in tune — subscription-based tech support centers that cater (in part) to small business owners. **Ask Dr. Tech**, one of the new breed's leaders, offers 24/7 tech support by phone, live chat or e-mail for PCs, Macs and peripherals of all the main makes and models, plus onsite repair. They can help you set up systems you just purchased, solve computer or software problems in a flash, or give a new employee valuable tips on using key business software. The $299 per year Business Plan subscription cost includes unlimited calls on the toll-free support line. Ask Dr. Tech also delivers automated diagnostic tools, system maintenance tools, business software support and more.

BizBest ActionGuide: See the site; call **(800) 275-3783**; or e-mail: info@askdrtech.com

---

Small Business Owners Ask...
About E-Commerce Solutions

Dear BizBest: *The rinky-dink shop doing my Web site looks shaky. Where can I get turnkey Web site and e-commerce services I can handle myself.* — Now a Do-It-Yourselfer

Bigstep
(www.bigstep.com)

Bigstep designs, hosts, manages and supports Web sites for thousands of small and home-based businesses — *exclusively*. This is one quick and easy place to get a Web site built and hosted, with personalized sales and lead generation services. You won't get the big fancy site of your dreams, but for something basic and functional from folks who cater to small biz, Bigstep has a proven track record and customer base. Package deals range from $15/month for Bigstep Basic to $55/month for a complete Bigstep Store with merchant account for credit card sales. Bigstep helps you focus less on tech and more on reaching customers. It's a one-stop source for building and managing a Web site, with automated e-commerce, marketing and promotion services created especially for small business.

★★★★	Focus on Small Biz
★★★★	Easy Accessibility
★★★★	Responsiveness
★★★	Vital to Growth
★★★	Value/Cost
★★★	Longevity

Best Feature: All-in-one service
Biggest Hangup: With luck, you may outgrow it.

BizBest ActionGuide: See the site or call **(866) 499-2799**.

CDW Computer Centers
(www.cdw.com)

★★★	Focus on Small Biz
★★★★	Easy Accessibility
★★★	Responsiveness
★★★★	Vital to Growth
★★★★	Value/Cost
★★★	Longevity

Best Feature: Your own rep
Biggest Hangup: Missing brands

Founded in 1984 as a home-based biz and based in Vernon Hills, IL, **CDW** has grown into a Fortune 500 company that specializes in direct sales of customized computer technology (hardware, software, networking devices) to small and mid-sized businesses. This is a place to shop for computers where the people actually understand small business and can help you build systems that can grow with your specific type of company. Nearly 96 percent of the company's more than $4 billion in annual sales come from business owner accounts. CDW has built strong relationships in the technology sector and is a leading direct source for many top brands (except for those that sell direct themselves, such as Dell). Something you don't get enough of these days: CDW offers individual *account managers* for one-on-one relationships, plus purchasing by fax, phone or online, custom-configured solutions, same-day shipping; flexible financing and phone or online tech support (with some 80 certified technicians). CDW's online SOLUTIONS LIBRARY is a helpful collection of articles that can help make any biz owner more tech savvy. Examine the pieces of information technology, explore data storage options and stay abreast of the latest tech.

BizBest ActionGuide: Call **(800) 838-4239**; e-mail: cdwsales@web.cdw.com

C/NET
(www.cnet.com)

Need software or hardware reviews? How about good leads on the best places to purchase tech for your biz? Or are you looking for software updates to download? **CNET** is a good spot for all of that, and more. **CNET Software**

★★	Focus on Small Biz
★★★★	Easy Accessibility
★★★	Responsiveness
★★★★	Vital to Growth
★★★★	Value/Cost
★★★	Longevity

Best Feature: Tech expertise
Biggest Hangup: Tech jargon

(**www.software.cnet.com**) is great for reliable software information, features, reviews, downloads and resource links. CNET Reviews has details and opinions on hundreds of tech products for small business. Be aware, however, that C/NET is a technology specialist, not a small business specialist, so the information tends to be more geared to techies. Still, the analysis is solid, easy to come by and can be applied to small business.

BizBest ActionGuide: You'll need to spend a little time exploring this rather massive site.

Dell Computer
(www.dell.com)

Dell is a technology dynamo that can put high-powered computers in your business for the least amount of money. Dell knows that biz

★★★★	Focus on Small Biz
★★★★	Easy Accessibility
★★★★	Responsiveness
★★★★	Vital to Growth
★★★★★	Value/Cost
★★★★	Longevity
Best Feature: Online ease	
Biggest Hangup: Only Dell stuff	

owners are super price conscious. So according to Frank Muehlman, who heads the company's small business division, Dell checks its prices against the competition every day. That kind of attention has made Dell one of the big biz suppliers considered most responsive to the needs of small companies and has earned it five *BizBest* stars for Value. Dell's selection is huge, with everything a small business might need by way of computers, software, peripherals, service and support. The "Buying Guide Center" (under Software & Peripherals) has helpful advice on what to get.

BizBest ActionGuide: At the Web site, click on "Small Business" or call **(800) 917-DELL**.

Intranets.com
(www.intranets.com)

★★★	Focus on Small Biz
★★★★	Easy Accessibility
★★★	Responsiveness
★★★	Vital to Growth
★★★	Value/Cost
★★★	Longevity
Best Feature: Free test drive	
Biggest Hangup: There's a learning curve	

Intranets.com is a great solution for today's growing legions of small businesses with "virtual" staff members who often work solo from their own offices. This application service provider (ASP) offers a secure, password-protected space on the Web where you, your partners, clients, remote workers, independent contractors or others can access and share documents, calendars and other information. Intranets.com has over 150,000 users worldwide. Because all your important business information resides in a central Web-based repository, it's available any time, from anywhere, using a simple Web browser. Basic rate is $49.95/month for the first five users and $9.95/month for each additional user. Free 30-day test drive available.

BizBest ActionGuide: See the site or call **(888) 932-2600**

Network Solutions
(www.networksolutions.com)

Network Solutions, Inc., the Web services giant that has registered over 15 million domains, is a supermarket of Internet services. They're not the lowest cost provider; you can register domains for less elsewhere. But they are likely to stick around, which translates into peace of mind for biz owners. Get e-mail, Web sites and a full range of Web site services all in one place. Their Web site builder software is great for do-it-yourself biz owners. You can build a simple site in half a day, or if you are willing to work at it longer, you can create a site with as many pages and features as you wish — all at an extremely reasonable cost. One cool e-mail feature we like, called "Catchall," lets you have an unlimited number of e-mail addresses attached to your domain for $10 per year. For example, if your domain is MyDomain.com and you've set up a mailbox for You@MyDomain.com, you can receive all mail addressed in ANY way, as long as it contains

★★★	Focus on Small Biz
★★★★	Easy Accessibility
★	Responsiveness
★★★★	Vital to Growth
★★★	Value/Cost
★★★	Longevity

Best Feature: Range of services
Biggest Hangup: Tech support severely lacking at times

@MyDomain.com. Great way to make a small biz appear bigger. **A word of caution**: NetSol's customer service flat out stinks at times, despite regular efforts to make improvements. Keep calling until you find a knowledgeable rep, or try their online customer service.

BizBest ActionGuide: Visit the Web site or call **(800) 779-1057**.

Small Business Owners Ask...
About Keeping Up With Tech

Dear BizBest: *I'm not a tech geek, but I still want to keep up with the latest technology tools, like computers, software and Internet applications for small business. Is there an easy way for us non-nerds to get the latest info quickly, and in plain English?* — Not a Nerd

Small Business Computing
(www.smallbusinesscomputing.com)

Dear Non-Nerd: A one-time print magazine called *Small Business Computing* crashed and burned but was reborn as an excellent Web site and e-newsletter under the same name. It's part of the **Internet.com** family of tech-related sites. Material is timely, insightful, super abundant and not overly technical for the non-geek business owner.

★★★★★	Focus on Small Biz
★★★★	Easy Accessibility
★★	Responsiveness
★★★	Vital to Growth
★★★	Value/Cost
★★	Longevity
Best Feature: Tons of material	
Biggest Hangup: You become hooked; get in too deep	

You'll find daily news, along with reviews, a buyers guide and extensive archives. This is good stuff for becoming — or staying — tech savvy, and best of all, it is all specifically geared to you as a small business owner, and free!

BizBest ActionGuide: Check out the Web site and sign up for the newsletter.

Small Business Owners Ask...
About Bar Codes

Dear BizBest: *I launched a mail order hot sauce business two years ago. Now we're growing and to get our product carried by other distributors we need a bar code. But I don't know a twit about them. Please help!* — Bar Code Challenged

Dear Challenged: Ah, yes, the ubiquitous bar code — also known as a Universal Product Code (UPC) or "automatic identification device." If your small business produces a product of almost any kind, you'll probably need to understand and make use of these handy little devices. Bar codes are also useful for tracking parts, inventory, coupons, invoices or documents. Here is our top pick for a vital site than can help make you a bar code expert.

Uniform Code Council, Inc.
(www.uc-council.org)

The 12-digit, all-numeric Universal Product Code (or bar code) identifies each product (as well as the company that makes it) warehoused, sold, delivered and billed through retail and wholesale channels. Here's the tricky part: You must become a "member" of the **Uniform Code Council, Inc.** (UCC) in order to obtain your very own numbers. But it's a two-step process. Once you have your numbers, you must still go to a commercial bar code vendor to produce the bar code symbols themselves. The UCC site explains it all. For quick answers, click on FAQs at the top of the page, then on UCC Member Organization FAQs.

★	Focus on Small Biz
★★★	Easy Accessibility
★★★	Responsiveness
★★★★	Vital to Growth
★★	Value/Cost
★★★★	Longevity

Best Feature: Step by step instructions
Biggest Hangup: Not geared to small biz

Step by step instructions are included, and you can apply for membership online or by phone. Cost is based on the number of products you have and your annual sales. To find bar code vendors, search the Solution Providers Directory under "Education and Support."

BizBest ActionGuide: Visit the Web site; call **(937) 435-3870**; e-mail info@uc-council.org.

Section 4

Sales & Marketing

★★★	Focus on Small Biz
★★★★★	Easy Accessibility
★★	Responsiveness
★★★	Vital to Growth
★★★★	Value/Cost
★★	Longevity

Best Feature: Find your info fast
Biggest Hangup: Can it survive?

Business.com

Business.com, "The Business Search Engine," is one of the best single Web destinations for business research. It's a free and biz-specific search engine designed to help you find the companies, products, services and marketing info you need for smart decisions. Site has some 400,000 listings in 25,000 industry, product and service categories. This ad-supported site skips the frills. Business.com's home page features a simple list of 25 industry categories, each divided into dozens more sub-categories. Customize your visits and monitor news by industry.

Also list your own site in the Business.com Network for $99 per year. Business.com listings appear on C/NET, Internet.com, BusinessWeek.com, Inc.com, FastCompany.com and others.

BizBest ActionGuide: Call **(310) 586-4111**.

Direct Marketing Association
(www.the-dma.org)

★	Focus on Small Biz
★★★★	Easy Accessibility
★★	Responsiveness
★★★★	Vital to Growth
★★★	Value/Cost
★★★★	Longevity
Best Feature: The publications	
Biggest Hangup: Big biz focus	

New York-based DMA is a giant industry association for business people of all kinds who are involved in direct marketing. The entire organization is about increasing direct mail effectiveness. Offers tons of training, publications, research, etc. DMA is the largest group for businesses interested in interactive and database marketing, with nearly 4,700 member companies from the U.S. and other nations. Members include direct marketers from every business segment as well as the non-profit and electronic marketing sectors — catalogers, Internet retailers and service providers, financial services providers, publishers, retailers, manufacturers and a host of other vertical segments.

BizBest ActionGuide: Publications are very helpful. Call **(212) 768-7277**; e-mail: membership@the-dma.org.

Hoover's, Inc.
(www.hoovers.com)

Hoover's is a terrific market research or competitive intelligence option for small biz owners who want to identify key decision-makers at U.S. companies, or if you need to identify potential threats and opportunities to your business, partners or customers. Hoover's doesn't merely regurgitate data, it creates its own unique insights and keeps its data religiously up-to-date. Hoover's is one of the few information providers offering an "editorialized" database. Rather than relying on company-produced information, its editors dig behind the scenes.

★	Focus on Small Biz
★★★★	Easy Accessibility
★★	Responsiveness
★★★★	Vital to Growth
★★★	Value/Cost
★★★★	Longevity
Best Feature: Info originality	
Biggest Hangup: Small universe	

The result is business intelligence that's more objective and reliable than most. Some basic info is available free (for example, you can browse A to Z company listings with address, phone and Web site); but most you pay for by subscription. A "Hoover's Lite" subscription — their lowest cost option — is $399/year or $49.95/month. This gets you access to an intelligence database listing about 21,000 companies and 180,000 key people in 600 industries.

BizBest ActionGuide: Visit the Web site or call **(866) 635-9715**.

Incentive Marketing Association
(www.incentivemarketing.org)

Need information on designing an incentive marketing or employee

★★★	Focus on Small Biz
★★★★	Easy Accessibility
★★★	Responsiveness
★★★	Vital to Growth
★★★★	Value/Cost
★★★★	Longevity
Best Feature: Easy access	
Biggest Hangup: Promotional	

motivation program for your business? The **Incentive Marketing Association** — a trade group for the incentive marketing industry — is the place to get the latest how-to and reference information on everything you need to know. It's a great resource for small business owners. The information is FREE (although you'll need to register), and covers topics such as business on the internet, direct marketing, employee motivation, event marketing, incentive travel, new business development, trade shows and training. There's an incentive supplier directory, detailed case studies, how-to articles, research and more.

BizBest ActionGuide: HQ: Naperville, IL. Call **(630) 369-7780**; e-mail: ima@IncentiveMarketing.org

InfoUSA
(www.infousa.com)

InfoUSA, Inc. is a huge source of sales leads and business or consumer mailing lists. Offers numerous business directories on CD-ROM, including directories for all 50 states, American big business (193,000 com-

★★★	Focus on Small Biz
★★★★	Easy Accessibility
★★★	Responsiveness
★★★	Vital to Growth
★★★	Value/Cost
★★★★	Longevity
Best Feature: Lists galore	
Biggest Hangup: Best if you know what you want	

panies), U.S. businesses of all sizes (11 million), manufacturers (645,000), doctors (575,000) and entrepreneurs (4.5 million). The site offers search functions to help you find what you need.

BizBest ActionGuide: Call: **(800) 321-0869.**

Small Business Owners Ask...
About Sales Networking

Dear BizBest: *My business needs a boost right now, and frankly so do I. I'd like to step up my networking with other business owners to gather ideas on growth, gain some support and maybe scare up leads or opportunities. Can you help plug me in?* — Feeling Lonely

Leads Club
(www.leadsclub.com)

Dear Lonely: Happy to do it. Business networking is always a good idea. And when times are tough, leads are lean or your cash is crunched, networking can be a terrific way to shake something loose and gather ideas about what others are doing. Leads Club has chapters across the U.S. and is open to biz owners, professionals, sales people and managers seeking to start or expand a business.

★★★★	Focus on Small Biz
★★	Easy Accessibility
★★★	Responsiveness
★★★★	Vital to Growth
★★★	Value/Cost
★★★	Longevity
Best Feature: It works	
Biggest Hangup: May not be available in your area	

At weekly breakfast or lunch meetings, members give a brief presentation and exchange leads. Meetings are run by and for the members with the only purpose being networking for referrals. Limit of one person per business category in a chapter. No time is spent on subjects which do not produce leads.

BizBest ActionGuide: Check the Web site for regional offices or call **(800) 783-3761.**

Small Business Owners Ask...

About Marketing Resources

Dear BizBest: *Like most owners of a new business, I can't afford to hire outside marketing experts. So, I'll simply have to become a marketing wizard myself. What are the best resources to get me there?* — Future Marketing Maven

Dear Future Maven: Who needs high-priced experts when you can become one yourself? Sure, it would be great to simply hire all the experts we need to run a successful business. But young companies often can't afford that, so a little "self-help" learning is the way to go. Here's a standout resources that can point you and your small business toward the marketing big leagues.

MarketingPower.com

★★★	Focus on Small Biz
★★★★	Easy Accessibility
★★★	Responsiveness
★★★	Vital to Growth
★★★★	Value/Cost
★★★	Longevity

Best Feature: Well organized
Biggest Hangup: Time consuming

MarketingPower.com is a super-useful marketing Web site created by the Chicago-based **American Marketing Association**. Although dues-paying AMA members (38,000 of them) get access to more content and discounts, there is a remarkable amount of helpful info available free. You'll find hundreds of articles on advertising, market research, consumer marketing, business-to-business marketing, Internet marketing and more. Sign up for free guides and Web casts by marketing experts. AMA's free demographics service (registration required) provides unlimited access to U.S. Census data on such things as home values and population trends. Get info right down to your local Zip Code. There is a helpful directory of marketing suppliers and excellent marketing tools and templates you can also access for free.

BizBest ActionGuide: Explore this powerful site to see all it offers. Call AMA at **(800) 262-1150**; e-mail info@ama.org.

SalesForce.com

★★	Focus on Small Biz
★★★	Easy Accessibility
★★★	Responsiveness
★★★★	Vital to Growth
★★★	Value/Cost
★★★	Longevity

Best Feature: Sophisticated
Biggest Hangup: Sophisticated

SalesForce.com can put the power of Web-based technology behind your sales, marketing and customer support efforts. The San Francisco-based firm works with both large and small businesses and delivers one of the Web's top, on-demand customer relationship management (CRM) services, including sales force automation, customer service/support and marketing automation. Salesforce.com is a utility-like service with nothing to install and minimal training to be up and running in days. Their *S3 Team Edition* product helps small teams of up to five people manage customer relationships for $995 per year.

BizBest ActionGuide: Call **(800) NO-SOFTWARE**; e-mail info@salesforce.com

★★★	Focus on Small Biz
★★★★	Easy Accessibility
★★★	Responsiveness
★★★	Vital to Growth
★★	Value/Cost
★★★★★	Longevity

Best Feature: Online search
Biggest Hangup: The cost

Thomas Register
(www.thomaspublishing.com)

Thomas Publishing, America's premier resource for industrial purchasing information, produces dozens of major buying guides on specialized industrial subjects, in print, CD-ROM and online formats. **Thomas Register** (**www.thomasregister.com**), which lists 173,000 U.S. and Canadian manufacturers, is a terrific source of info on industrial products and services. The Web site offers extensive company and product details, RFQ's for thousands of manufacturers, plus online catalogs and links to company Web sites. STANDOUT FEATURE: Good search capabilities, by product, service, company or brand. **Thomas Regional Directory (www.thomasregional.com)** helps connect industrial buyers and sellers in local markets across the country. This industrial search engine offers instant access to a database of 550,000 distributors, manufacturers and service companies. Find companies by product or service, type of company, location, trade names or other specifications.

BizBest ActionGuide: Visit the Web sites or call **(800) 699-9822.**

Trade Show News Network
(www.tsnn.com)

Trade Show News Network calls itself "The Ultimate Trade Show Resource." And they're probably right. At this comprehensive site you'll find info on more than 15,000 trade shows and conferences, listed by industry (agriculture, apparel, antiques, etc.) and great advice on

★★	Focus on Small Biz
★★★★	Easy Accessibility
★★	Responsiveness
★★★	Vital to Growth
★★★★	Value/Cost
★★★	Longevity
Best Feature: Comprehensive	
Biggest Hangup: Big biz, too	

trade show planning, logistics, convention centers, travel, online service providers, virtual trade shows, international shows, sales, marketing and much more. Needham, MA-based **TSNN** is a high-octane small biz resource for anything to do with trade shows.

BizBest ActionGuide: Call **(781) 449-0286**; e-mail: info@tsnn.com

---

Small Business Owners Ask...
About Direct Mail

Dear BizBest: *I'd like to promote my business with direct mail, but I'm in the dark. Where do I go to get it done right?*
— In the Dark

★★★★	Focus on Small Biz
★★★★	Easy Accessibility
★★★	Responsiveness
★★★★	Vital to Growth
★★★★	Value/Cost
★★★	Longevity
Best Feature: Turnkey service	

Zairmail
(www.zairmail.com)

Dear In The Dark: Despite the lure of e-commerce and e-mail marketing, direct mail remains one of the most tried-and-true small business marketing methods. And there are terrific new ways to combine high tech with old-fashioned mailings. **Zairmail** is a nifty Web-based service that lets you send personalized direct mail to customers via your PC. With this turnkey service, you can quickly do online what once took weeks using traditional printing and production. Compose your document and let Zairmail guide you through the process. No special software or experience needed.

BizBest ActionGuide: Call **(877) 921-MAIL**; e-mail info@zairmail.com

---

Section **5**

Operations

AOL for Small Business
(www.AOLforsmallbusiness.com)

★★★★★	Focus on Small Biz
★★★★	Easy Accessibility
★★★★	Responsiveness
★★★	Vital to Growth
★★★★	Value/Cost
★	Longevity

Best Feature: Customer service
Biggest Hangup: Still new

Many small biz owners started with AOL service, but quickly graduated to business class e-mail and Web access. **AOL for Small Business** may halt that exodus. It's a special version of AOL that gives you access to first-rate small business "how-to" information, business e-mail, Web sites, discounts on products and services, and much more. If you already have AOL there is no additional charge, but you have to sign up. Great feature: 24/7 business-class priority customer service by chat, e-mail or phone.

BizBest ActionGuide: Go to **www.AOLforsmallbusiness.com** or AOL Keyword: Small Business. Call: **(877) 265-7200**.

★★	Focus on Small Biz
★★★★	Easy Accessibility
★★★	Responsiveness
★★★	Vital to Growth
★★★★	Value/Cost
★★★	Longevity

Best Feature: Time-saving tips
Biggest Hangup: Undergoing redesign at this writing

BizTraveler.org

Biztraveler.org, from the **National Business Travel Association** (NBTA), is an excellent, free resource for news and tips on biz travel that can save you time and money and make business travel easier and more productive. This is info from biz travel insiders and experts who've "been there, done that." NBTA (**www.nbta.org**) is a membership group for corporate travel managers and biz travel service providers. But if your small biz is travel-intensive, the $345 annual dues may be worth it. NBTA can tip you off on money-saving biz travel tactics and situations to avoid.

BizBest ActionGuide: Call Alexandria, VA-based NBTA at **(703) 684-0836**.

Energy Star, Small Business
(www.energystar.gov/smallbiz)

Simply put, if your small biz spends money on energy, the **Energy Star** program can put money in your pocket. Hundreds of small firms are saving thousands per year thanks to the services and advice they got here. Yes, **Energy Star** is run by the U.S. Environmental Protection Agency (EPA). But don't let

★★★★★	Focus on Small Biz
★★★	Easy Accessibility
★★★★	Responsiveness
★	Vital to Growth
★★★★	Value/Cost
★★★★	Longevity

Best Feature: Payback
Biggest Hangup: Investment

that put you off. This independent program is well run and helps small business save money on energy costs with all kinds of technical help, support services and resources. By signing up, you'll receive a How-To guide for analyzing and upgrading your facility, lists of energy equipment and service contractors, access to free workshops and even public relations materials to promote your efforts. Members agree to implement a plan, but only when it is profitable with a simple payback of three years or less. No reporting required, but if you tell Energy Star about your successful upgrade you'll receive special public recognition. Read some of the small biz success stories at the Web site.

BizBest ActionGuide: The FAQ section at the Web site is especially informative. Call **(888) STAR-YES**.

Kinko's
(www.kinkos.com)

★★★★★	Focus on Small Biz
★★★★	Easy Accessibility
★★★★	Responsiveness
★★★★	Vital to Growth
★★★★	Value/Cost
★★★★	Longevity

Best Feature: Small biz focus and 24/7 service

Kinko's is synonymous with small business. Countless biz owners worldwide consider their local **Kinko's** outlet an extension of their own companies. **Why?** Because Kinko's provides so many services vital to small business operations, and in many cases is there to serve you 24/7. From your first business cards and stationery, to a full range of copying, printing, online printing, signs, banners, shipping supplies/services, awards & trophies, photo enlargements, computer rental, meeting services and even videoconferencing, Kinko's has it covered. The company started in 1970 as a single copy shop. Today its network of some 1,200 digitally-connected locations is fully tech savvy, and can deliver all the color printing, presentation services, Web access and document management solutions entrepreneurs need to succeed. Order online to save time. Pickup in as little as four hours. You can pay online or at the branch. Kinko's even offers a free software tool that ensures your fonts, margins and graphics print as they appear on your screen. Kinko's "gets" small business.

BizBest ActionGuide: BONUS: Automatic 10% discount with Amex Business Card. Call: **(800) 2-KINKOS**; e-mail customerrelations@kinkos.com.

Manufacturing Extension Partnership
(www.mep.nist.gov)

MEP is a potential gold mine for small manufacturers. The sole purpose of this national network of 400 not-for-profit centers is to help small manufacturing firms become more productive, tech-savvy and competitive. *BizBest* has tracked this program for near-

★★★★★	Focus on Small Biz
★★	Easy Accessibility
★★★	Responsiveness
★★★★	Vital to Growth
★★★★	Value/Cost
★★★	Longevity

Best Feature: Hands on help
Biggest Hangup: Locations

ly 10 years and has found it to be well-run and highly beneficial for biz owners who've used it. You can tap MEP's army of experts for help in many areas, from improving plant layout to getting your shop floor in shape to restructuring your finances, designing a Web site or entering e-commerce. The cost is a fraction of what you'd pay private consultants. MEP centers, serving all 50 States, make it possible for even the smallest firms to tap top-level manufacturing and business specialists with experience in manufacturing. *If you are in manufacturing, don't miss this great resource.*

BizBest ActionGuide: Calling **(800) 637-4634** routs you to the MEP center for your region. Reach HQ at **(301) 975-5020**. The Web site offers a full view of the program, plus success stories and a list of MEP affiliates.

Office Business Center Association
(www.officebusinesscenters.com)

★★	Focus on Small Biz
★★★★	Easy Accessibility
★★★	Responsiveness
★★★★	Vital to Growth
★★★	Value/Cost
★★★	Longevity
Best Feature: Short term space in 600 cities	

OBCA can help you find turn-key business space in over 600 cities worldwide. Office business centers (executive office suites) are a great way for a small biz to establish itself in a professional environment with shared services (receptionist, conference rooms, copiers, etc.) at a reasonable cost. Offices are generally available by the hour, day, week, month or year. Most centers provide Web access and concierge-type handling of business needs, including travel, videoconferencing, mobile messaging, desktop publishing, telemarketing, catering, law libraries, computer networking, consulting, training and more.

BizBest ActionGuide: HQ: Columbus, OH; Call: **(800) 237-4741**; (614) 985-3633; e-mail info@officebusinesscenters.com

Office Depot
(www.officedepot.com)

★★★★	Focus on Small Biz
★★★★	Easy Accessibility
★★★	Responsiveness
★★★★	Vital to Growth
★★★★	Value/Cost
★★★★	Longevity
Best Feature: Small biz friendly with great deals.	

In the colossally-competitive category of office supplies, **Office Depot** has achieved standout status for small business, home office and startup solutions. When the issue is catering to small biz, Office Depot is one of the big companies that seems to "get it." A preferred customer program can get you additional discounts on already-low prices on in-store purchases.

For busy biz owners, the Web site is a huge time-saver, and a valuable source of solutions and info. Order $50 or more online and receive free shipping. Delivery at your door in a day or two. Site offers handy product comparisons and a **Your Business Center** section that can be personalized to your needs as a small biz owner. You'll find free forms and templates you can download (like job reference forms, a daily cash sheet and customer satisfaction survey), plus a small business handbook with helpful articles, a Web resource directory and links to other solution providers such as bCentral for Web hosting, as well as a print center, tech support and Internet postage. The search tools work great and can find you what you need in an instant.

BizBest ActionGuide: Open an account online at **www.officedepot.com** or call **(888) 463-3768**.

Small Business Owners Ask...
About Postal Solutions

Dear BizBest: *Business is slow so I'm stepping up my mailings. One problem, though: we're still using stick-on stamps, and the hassles are making me come unglued. I know there are better ways, like Internet postage. Help!*
— Unglued

Pitney Bowes/PitneyWorks
(www.pitneyworks.com)

★★★★★ Focus on Small Biz	
★★★★ Easy Accessibility	
★★★★ Responsiveness	
★★★★ Vital to Growth	
★★★★ Value/Cost	
★★★★ Longevity	
Best Feature: 24/7 postage	

Dear Unglued: Time to join the 21st Century! ClickStamp Internet Postage is the online postage service from meter maven **Pitney Bowes**. All you need is a computer, printer and Internet connection to print your own postage for letters and packages. Works for all types of mail, including First-Class, Priority, Express and Parcel Post. Integrates with Microsoft Word and other software to print postage directly on envelopes. Postage available 24/7 so you'll never run out. Costs $4.99 per month, plus the postage. If you prefer to meter your mail, Pitney has a full line of equipment and services. Their Personal Post, for example, is great for small biz. Plug it into a phone line and get postage refills with the touch of a button. Pitney makes a concerted effort to serve and understand small business. **PitneyWorks.com** is its main small biz outlet and an excellent place to find mailing and shipping solutions. The Shipping and Tracking Tool is a free service that helps you track packages, look up ZIP codes and determine the best way to ship packages and overnight letters. The free **ValueShip** feature will help you find the least expensive way to get your package delivered in the fastest time. Just fill out the online form and ValueShip will shop your shipment among Airborne, FedEx, the Postal Service and others.

BizBest ActionGuide: Visit **www.pitneyworks.com** or call **(800) 390-0297.**

Quikbook
(www.quikbook.com)

★★	Focus on Small Biz
★★★★	Easy Accessibility
★★★★	Responsiveness
★★	Vital to Growth
★★★★★	Value/Cost
★★★	Longevity

Best Feature: Sleeps there too
Biggest Hangup: More cities!

Forget those giant discount travel Web sites with their complex rules and spotty results. Some of the most savvy, bargain-conscious small business travelers turn to **Quikbook** when they want a premium hotel room at 20 to 60 percent off in more than a hundred cities in North America. BizBest CEO Daniel Kehrer first used Quikbook shortly after it began in 1988, offering rooms only in New York. Now Quikbook is everywhere, from Albuquerque, NM to Worcester, MA, specializing in great hotels at great prices. Customer service is exceptional, and the Quikbook folks pride themselves on their knowledge of each hotel, because they visit each one. The Web site is a breeze to navigate.

BizBest ActionGuide: Visit quikbook.com or call **(800) 789-9887.**

United Parcel Service (UPS)
(www.ups.com)

In a survey conducted yearly since 1987 by Cicco & Associates, a market research firm in Murrysville, PA, biz owners are asked to name large companies that are *particularly responsive to the needs of small business*. Right on top is **United Parcel Service**. UPS has

★★★★★	Focus on Small Biz
★★★★★	Easy Accessibility
★★★★	Responsiveness
★★★★	Vital to Growth
★★★★	Value/Cost
★★★★	Longevity

Best Feature: Internet options are great for small biz

the shipping thing nailed, with programs for small business that make the process super efficient. Their Internet options work like the proverbial well-oiled machine. Log in, print out your shipping label and alert UPS to your pickup, all with a few clicks. And surprise! UPS is also a source of small biz loans. An Atlanta-based unit called **UPS Capital** has quietly become one of the top ten small biz lenders in America. While traditional financial institutions tend to run hot and cold on small biz, small companies have always been big customers for UPS and the firm remains committed through good times and bad. A new UPS service called **On-Call Pickup** is great for busy biz owners. For next-day pickup requests placed online, the cost is only $2. Same-day service is $4; or $5 if you request by phone. You can quickly prepare packages for shipment using your own computer and printer through **MyUPS.com**. Or call **(800) PICK-UPS**.

BizBest ActionGuide: Call **(800) PICK-UPS** or open an account online at **www.ups.com**. UPS Capital visit **www.upscapital.com**; call **(800) 637-0620**.

U.S. Postal Service
Direct Mail Site
(www.usps.com/directmail)

★★★★★	Focus on Small Biz
★★★★	Easy Accessibility
★★★	Responsiveness
★★★	Vital to Growth
★★★★	Value/Cost
★★★★	Longevity

Best Feature: Provider links
Biggest Hangup: Does everything but sell your stuff

The **USPS** has a super-helpful direct mail Web site just for small biz. You'll find good advice and links to service providers who offer complete online solutions for direct mail campaigns, from list services to creative, print, production and mail entry. *This is basically all most small businesses will need to launch a direct mail campaign.* There are also helpful tutorials, templates you can adapt to your own campaign and a list of "Direct Mail Made Easy" seminars if you're in the mood for learning even more. This is a complete, easy to grasp package from the P.O.

BizBest ActionGuide: Go to **www.usps.com/directmail**. For a list of contact phone numbers go to www.usps.com/common/contact_us.

Section **6**

Money & Finance

CIT Small Business Lending Corp.
(www.smallbizlending.com)

★★★★★	Focus on Small Biz
★★★	Easy Accessibility
★★★	Responsiveness
★★★	Vital to Growth
★★★★	Value/Cost
★★★	Longevity

Best Feature: Lots of loans
Biggest Hangup: They make you pay it back

New York-based **CIT Small Business Lending Corporation**, a unit of CIT Group Inc., is the largest Small Business Administration (SBA) lender in the U.S., doling out nearly $800 million in small biz loans annually to more than 1,500 small businesses nationwide. CIT outpaces its nearest rival by more than $250 million in SBA loans. And John Canning, president of CIT Small Business Lending, certainly talks the small biz talk: "Our goal is to continue helping entrepreneurs realize their dreams of starting, owning and growing their businesses," he says. But his company also walks the walk by making SBA-backed small business loans easier to apply for than ever before. CIT is also an SBA "Preferred Lender" in most states, which means it can provide quicker credit decisions and loan closings. Loans range from $50,000 to $3 million for all kinds of small businesses, including: restaurants, physicians, dentists, veterinarians, franchise hotels, funeral homes, assisted living facilities and day care centers. Offers loans for business acquisition and expansion, commercial real estate, construction and franchise start-ups and re-sales.

BizBest ActionGuide: The Web site has a helpful *EZScreen*, online SBA screening application that can give you a quick read on whether you're a good candidate for a loan, plus articles on how to present a good application. You can apply online or call **(800) 713-4984**.

Small Business Owners Ask...
About Cutting Costs

Dear BizBest: *Like many business owners, I'm pinching pennies these days. Where can I find cost-cutting ideas as well as discount deals on routine purchases like shipping, insurance, software, printing and computers?* — Pinching Pennies

Cost Blaster
(www.costblaster.com)

★★★★	Focus on Small Biz
★★★	Easy Accessibility
★	Responsiveness
★★★	Vital to Growth
★★★★	Value/Cost
★★	Longevity

Best Feature: Long list of cost-cutting leads and links
Biggest Hangup: No way to contact them.

Dear Penny Pincher: Cost **Blaster** is a small business resource that BizBest considers to be a "Hidden Gem." This little known site is uncluttered, easy to grasp and chock full of cost-cutting and money-saving leads and links. Categories include payroll, phones, insurance, rent, marketing, travel, printing, shipping, supplies and accounting.

BizBest ActionGuide: Visit the Web site or e-mail staff@costblaster.com. No phone contact.

D&B Small Business Solutions
(sbs.dnb.com)

The old Dun & Bradstreet, now simply **D&B,** offers business credit and background reports, marketing services (sales leads; mailing lists), research and risk-management prod-

★★★★★	Focus on Small Biz
★★★★	Easy Accessibility
★★★★	Responsiveness
★★★	Vital to Growth
★★★	Value/Cost
★★★★★	Longevity
Best Feature: Biz credit reports	
Biggest Hangup: Costs add up	

ucts for small business via a unit called **D&B Small Business Solutions (SBS)**. You'll find D&B best in four key areas: 1) Checking background and credit worthiness of other businesses; 2) Building or monitoring *your own* business credit (see *CreditBuilder* and *SelfMonitor*); 3) help with collections; and 4) B2B marketing. Doing deals with other companies? D&B background and credit reports can help you make decisions. Or if you regularly grant credit, D&B services are vital. Memberships offered at various levels, from free to a Gold $40/month package. Credit eValuator Reports are available for over 13 million businesses. Call: **(866) 472-7362** or **(866) 584-0248**. D&B also offers pay-as-you-go plans that let you tap reports with a phone call or online. D&B will also alert you by e-mail if the credit status of one of your customers changes. Receivable Management Services can help you recoup uncollected balances. **D&B Marketing Services** can help you identify and reach new customers and get the most out of relationships with existing customers. Click "Marketing Services" at the Web site. Call **(866) 719-7158**. D&B also has an extensive minority- and women-owned business database.

BizBest ActionGuide: Visit the Web site or call **(800) 396-9090**.

Equipment Leasing Association
(www.elaonline.com)

The **Equipment Leasing Association** has a Web site called *Lease Assistant* (**www.leaseassistant.org**) covering all the basic questions — why consider leasing, benefits, what you can lease, how to evaluate leasing options — plus an excellent glossary of terms for those of us challenged by leasing jargon. If your biz is considering leasing, the info here can help you

★★	Focus on Small Biz
★★★★	Easy Accessibility
★★★	Responsiveness
★★	Vital to Growth
★★★	Value/Cost
★★★	Longevity
Best Feature: Leasing basics	
Biggest Hangup: Pro leasing	

make an informed decision. Just remember it comes from the leasing folks themselves. *Lease Assistant* has practical info about the mechanics of equipment leasing and financing, including case studies, what to ask when negotiating a lease and info on finding and selecting a leasing company.

BizBest ActionGuide: HQ: Arlington, VA; Call: **(703) 527-8655**.

FileTaxes.com
(www.filetaxes.com)

★★★	Focus on Small Biz
★★★★	Easy Accessibility
★★★	Responsiveness
★★★	Vital to Growth
★★★★	Value/Cost
★★	Longevity
Best Feature: Speed	
Biggest Hangup: Limited scope	

FileTaxes.com is an online tax filing service from **Greatland Corp**. Thousands of biz owners use it instead of buying software, filling out forms, making copies and mailing returns. File W-2, 1099 and 941 forms online in three easy steps: 1) Set up an account; 2) Fill in government-approved forms on your screen; 3) Click "submit." Your info goes to FileTaxes, which forwards data to the Feds and, for W-2s and 1099s, prints a copy of each and mails it to the recipient or employee. You also receive an e-mail confirmation for each filing. You can print a copy of any form filed to keep for your records or to file with state or local agencies. Access your database of filed forms at any time. Cost is $3.49 per form filed. Greatland (**www.greatland.com**) has 50 years experience in tax form development and works with 100,000 accountants and businesses.

BizBest ActionGuide: Call **(800) 968-1099**; Greatland's at www.greatland.com

Health Insurance Association of America
(www.hiaa.org)
Insurance Information Institute
(www.iii.org)

★	Focus on Small Biz
★★★	Easy Accessibility
★★	Responsiveness
★★	Vital to Growth
★★★	Value/Cost
★★★	Longevity
Best Feature: Insurance basics	
Biggest Hangup: One-sided	

HIAA, based in Washington, DC, and **III**, based in New York, are two separate organizations we've lumped into a single BizBest 100 listing. Need basic, accurate information about small business health insurance plans that isn't slanted toward one company or type of plan? The **Health Insurance Association of**

America (HIAA) offers a helpful online guidebook called the *Insurance Guide for Business Owners*. It's free at the HIAA Web site under Consumer Information (Guides). Covers small group health insurance, commercial insurance options, tips on choosing quality coverage and a handy checklist that helps you evaluate the type of coverage that will work best for your biz and the kinds of things you want covered and the coverage you can afford. A list of questions to ask is also valuable: For example: What is the total cost of the policy (including premium for employer and employee, co-insurance, maximum out-of-pocket, etc.)? Is the rate guaranteed? How long does it take to process claims? What will happen to premiums if one employee has a major claim? Other guides of interest include: Employer's Guide to Disability Income Insurance; Employer's Guide to Long-Term Care Insurance; and Guide to Medical Savings Accounts(MSA)/High Deductible Health Plans.

The **Insurance Information Institute** has plain-English answers to these questions (and more): How do I find the right agent? How can I save money on my business insurance? How do I insure my home business? What does a business owner's policy cover? Do I need business interruption insurance? How can I disaster-proof my business? How do I file a business insurance claim? What's the difference between cancellation and non-renewal? Do I need workers compensation insurance? Can I insure the life of a key employee? Do I need professional liability insurance? Do I need a commercial auto insurance policy? What is employment practices liability insurance (EPLI)? Click on "Business" at the Web site (a little confusing since it is listed under "Individuals."

BizBest ActionGuide: HIAA: **(888) 844-2782**: III: **(212) 346-5500**

InsuranceNoodle
(www.insurancenoodle.com)
InsuranceNoodle is an online insurance agency specializing in small business lines from major companies such as AIG, Chubb, CNA Surety, The Hartford, Philadelphia, Safeco, The St. Paul, XL Specialty and Zurich U.S. Offers insurance products for 200 specific types of small business. Get free

★★★★★	Focus on Small Biz
★★★★	Easy Accessibility
★★★★	Responsiveness
★★	Vital to Growth
★★★★	Value/Cost
★★	Longevity
Best Feature: Comparing quotes	
Biggest Hangup: Human touch	

quotes; make quick and easy policy comparisons online for business owner policies, commercial auto, workers' comp, umbrella insurance, employment practices liability and others.

BizBest ActionGuide: Call **(888) 466-6353**; e-mail info@insurancenoodle.com

Intuit / QuickBooks
(www.intuit.com) / (www.quickbooks.com)

Intuit's family of *QuickBooks* accounting software and payroll products and services are the standard-setters for helping small business owners manage finances, payroll, taxes and other money matters. *QuickBooks* (basic tools); *QuickBooks Pro* (more advanced); *QuickBooks Premier* (even more comprehensive); *QuickBooks Online Edition* (works over the Web); *Quickbooks Payroll Services* (do-it-yourself tools to full-serve solutions); point of sale software, online billing and other services offer the fastest, simplest ways to run the financial side of your business. The *QuickBooks* Web site is also an excellent source of information and advice on financial and tax matters that affect small business.

★★★★★ Focus on Small Biz
★★★★ Easy Accessibility
★★★★ Responsiveness
★★★★★ Vital to Growth
★★★★ Value/Cost
★★★★ Longevity
Best Feature: Sets the standard for small biz with expanding product line & support

QuickBooks now offers vertical products just for accountants, contractors, healthcare practices, retailers and nonprofits. For solo operators, the Quicken Home & Business product lets you manage both your business and personal finances separately (or together), from the same program. **Outstanding Web site features**: The QuickBooks Solutions Marketplace features some 300 other business applications that work with *Quickbook*. The "Compare Products" section gives you a quick view of how the various software products differ. A long menu of "Add-on" software and services includes tracking for time and billing, supply chain management, remote data backup, accounting advice and online banking.

BizBest ActionGuide: At **www.intuit.cim** click on "Small Business" for a menu of Intuit's small business products & services. Quickbooks info at **www.quickbooks.com** or call **(888) 246-8848** Payroll product info at **www.payroll.com** or call **(800) 624-2106**.

Small Business Owners Ask...
About Credit & Collections

Dear BizBest: *Blame it on the bad economy, but more of my clients are slow paying these days. I need resources on how to avoid collection problems and on finding and using a collection agency.* — Stuck with Tab

National Assn. of Credit Mgmt.
(www.nacm.org)

Dear Stuck: Ah, getting paid. It's an age-old problem for small biz owners, and one that never seems to go away.

★★★	Focus on Small Biz
★★★★	Easy Accessibility
★★★	Responsiveness
★★★	Vital to Growth
★★★	Value/Cost
★★★	Longevity

Best Feature: Forms & pubs
Biggest Hangup: Bigger biz focus

A slow economy makes it even worse. The **National Assn. of Credit Management**, a Columbia, Maryland-based trade group for biz people who deal with credit and collections, provides credit info and services to over 30,000 members. NACM offers many helpful publications about collections for business, along with credit forms you can use for your own credit customers.

BizBest ActionGuide: Visit the Web site or call **(410) 740-5560.**

OPEN: The Small Business Network
(open.americanexpress.com)

The OPEN network, an **American Express** creation, offers small biz owners an impressive array of helpful financial management tools, services and savings, including access to working capital and credit info and discounts on business products and services — including small business loans and credit lines. Membership is automatic when you apply for an American

★★★★★	Focus on Small Biz
★★★★★	Easy Accessibility
★★★★	Responsiveness
★★★	Vital to Growth
★★★★	Value/Cost
★★★★	Longevity

Best Features: Discounts and access to credit

Express Business Card for your small business. The 2002 rollout of OPEN was the first time American Express ever created separate branding for one of its business units — a big deal for a big company like Amex. You get automatic discounts at Kinko's (10%), FedEx (5-20%), select D&B credit services (20%), AOL Yellow Pages (50% on 6-month listing), Exxon (2%), Mobil (2%), Hertz (up to 20%), Hilton (10%), Dell (5%) and others. See the complete list in the EVERYDAY SAVINGS section of the Web site. Use the INFORM section of the site to find answers on subjects such as managing employees, finance, insurance, startup and others. In the CONNECT section you can network with other biz owners via Abuzz, a knowledge-sharing community run by *The New York Times*. You pose a question and other biz owners answer (online or via e-mail). Just sign up; the program is FREE and operates 24/7. Be sure to sign up for the MEMBERSHIP REWARDS program which earns you points for all your spending that can be redeemed dozens of ways, including airline tickets and various products.

BizBest ActionGuide: Visit the Web site or call **(800) NOW-OPEN**.

★★★★★	Focus on Small Biz
★★★★	Easy Accessibility
★★★★	Responsiveness
★★★★	Vital to Growth
★★★★	Value/Cost
★★★★	Longevity

Best Feature: A time-saver every small biz employer should have

Paychex
(www.paychex.com)

When small biz owners first started outsourcing more tasks back in the 1970s, one of the first was the time-consuming chore of doing payroll, and its associated tax filings. Tom Golisano started **Paychex** in 1971 with $3,000 and a good idea of how to make it easy and affordable for small businesses to outsource their payroll processing. Today the company is tops in providing not just payroll services to small biz owners, but also payroll tax administration, 401(k) plans, Section 125 plans and Workers' Comp insurance. And Paychex popularity shows, as the company now has over $1 billion in revenues. For those new to payroll, the Web site has an excellent introduction to what's involved in the process. Click "Business Owners" and then "Managing Your Payroll." Has 100 offices.

BizBest ActionGuide: Call **(800) 322-7292**; See site for office locations map

★★★★	Focus on Small Biz
★★★	Easy Accessibility
★★★	Responsiveness
★★★	Vital to Growth
★★★	Value/Cost
★★	Longevity

Best Feature: VC listings
Biggest Hangup: Still hard to get VC backing

Vfinance.com

At this biz finance portal you can post a synopsis of your idea, research lists of lenders, investment banks and angel investors and get leads on venture capital sources, accountants, lawyers, insurance providers and others. Some information is free, while other items involve a cost. Check out the **Venture Capital Resource Directory**. Since 1995, vfinance has researched and validated nearly all of the best-known VC firms in America. The list is constantly updated, checked for accuracy and free. Or an available VC search tool can help narrow your search and deliver detailed contact info tailored to your specific criteria (cost starts at $1.25 each).

BizBest ActionGuide: Visit the Web site or call **(561) 981-1017**

Wells Fargo
(www.wellsfargo.com/biz)

Wells Fargo — an exceptionally small business-friendly bank — has become the single most popular bank among biz owners since the mid 1990s. You can open accounts and apply for loans online or by mail, without visiting a branch, from just about anywhere in the country. "Small business is a real core priority for us," says Rebecca Macieira-Kaufmann, who heads the bank's small biz division. At **www.wellsfargo.com/biz,** you can apply for a loan, check insurance quotes, manage accounts, shop for small biz

★★★★★	Focus on Small Biz
★★★★★	Easy Accessibility
★★★	Responsiveness
★★★	Vital to Growth
★★★★	Value/Cost
★★★★	Longevity

Best Feature: Nationwide availability

services and more. The "Credit Product Finder" in the "Tools & Calculators" section is a super-helpful device for finding the right loan or line of credit for your type of business and location. The "Resources" section has a collection of business tips, advice on using *QuickBooks* accounting software and information about special Wells Fargo loan programs for women and minority business owners.

BizBest ActionGuide: Visit the Web site or call **(800) 225-5935** and press "0" to speak with a national business banker.

Section 7

Communications

Small Business Owners Ask...

About Phone Systems

Dear BizBest: *Our wimpy phone system handles the basics, but I want high-tech features that make my small biz sound bigger without having to install a big, new, expensive system. Ideas? — Phone Wimp*

Angel.com

Dear Phone Wimp: An up-and-coming Web-based service called Angel.com may be just the thing you're looking for. Angel offers voice recognition phone applications you can customize to your biz starting at $9.95/month, no hardware needed. Angel can answer your phones, provide info, transfer calls and take messages among dozens of features. Your biz is assigned a toll-free number. A customer calls and asks for anyone by name. The call is forwarded or a voice mail taken. You

★★★★	Focus on Small Biz
★★★★	Easy Accessibility
★★★	Responsiveness
★★★	Vital to Growth
★★★★	Value/Cost
★	Longevity
Best Feature: Free 30-day trial	
Biggest Hangup: Still new	

can be notified of the message by e-mail and check messages online from any PC. Angel also offers turnkey small business solutions for automating your sales and marketing; customer service and support and e-commerce, as well as audio production and voice talent services that can give you high quality prompts and clever audio elements you never considered. Hear samples of how Angel services work at www.angel.com. There's a free 30-day (50 minute) trial.

BizBest ActionGuide: Call **(888) MyAngel**; e-mail info@angle.com

Small Business Owners Ask...
About Cool 800 Numbers

Dear BizBest: I want a cool toll-free number that spells my business name. Is it hard to get? — Wanna Be Cool

★★★	Focus on Small Biz
★★★★★	Easy Accessibility
★★★★	Responsiveness
★★★	Vital to Growth
★★★★★	Value/Cost
★★★★	Longevity

Best Feature: Easy to check available numbers quickly

ATT.com

Dear Wanna Be: A toll-free number (800, 888, 877 or 866) is a great, yet inexpensive marketing and sales tool for even the smallest of businesses. Numbers that also spell the most popular words, like **800-SUCCESS** (which belongs to American Express Small Business), are long gone. You can avoid lengthy calls inquiring about number availability by checking numbers you are interested in online. A great place to do that is **www.att.com**, even if you don't use AT&T services (phone firms all draw from the same number pool). Click on Small & Medium Business; then on Toll-Free Service to search available numbers. Using a "wildcard" (the star ∗ symbol), makes it easy to find word combos. Say you want to spell the word FOOD in your number. Enter FOOD∗∗∗ to see available numbers where the first four digits spell FOOD and the last three could be any numbers (wildcards). It's simple to search, and kind of fun, too.

★★★	Focus on Small Biz
★★★★	Easy Accessibility
★★★	Responsiveness
★★★	Vital to Growth
★★	Value/Cost
★★★★	Longevity

Best Feature: MediaSource
Biggest Hangup: A bit pricey

Bacon's Information
(www.bacons.com)

Need media contacts for a PR push by mail, e-mail or fax? Chicago-based **Bacon's** has the best media directories around. The print versions of these babies aren't cheap — they range from $250 to $325 — but they're good. Separate editions published in categories such as: Newspapers & Magazines, Radio/TV/Cable, Internet, Computer & High Tech, Medical & Health, Business, International, and others. Since print guides go stale quickly, consider Bacon's online services that can provide media connections updated daily. Bacon's MediaLists Online (www.medialistsonline.com) is a simple online tool that lets you generate up-to-date media contact lists and labels in minutes right from your PC. Great for biz owners who do their own PR. But costs mount quickly. Small firms that spend over $2,000 per year on P.R. lists and mailings should consider **MediaSource**, Bacon's premium service. It's a powerful Web-based application that lets you research the media, build targeted contact lists and even distribute press releases or announcements via e-mail 24/7. *BizBest* road-tested MediaSource Internet (there is also a CD service) and found it easy to use and worthwhile. Cost is about $2,250/year, but the ability to blast as many e-mails and faxes as you like (up to 1,000 at a time) to media outlets at no additional cost can be worth the subscription price alone.

BizBest ActionGuide: See the Web site or call: **(877) 922-2400**. For MediaLists Online visit **www.medialistsonline.com**. You can also buy ready-to-use media lists or get turnkey service from **Bacon's Distribution Services** (**800-776-3342**). Tell 'em what you want; they'll handle it all.

Business Wire
(www.businesswire.com)

★★★	Focus on Small Biz
★★★★	Easy Accessibility
★★★	Responsiveness
★★★	Vital to Growth
★★★	Value/Cost
★★★	Longevity

Best Feature: Quick PR releases
Biggest Hangup: Can't guarantee you ink

Business Wire — a global leader in business news distribution — can deliver your small business press release simultaneously to media, analysts and financial professionals, online communities and targeted audiences based on your specifications. Business Wire's broadcast fax service, *NewsFax*, lets you distribute news releases and other documents to your private contact lists. Business Wire scans your letterhead into the system so it appears on all of your faxed documents. A 12-month membership is $120 and gives you 24/7 access to Business Wire experts and services to help you make the most of your PR dollars. A 400-word release to Business Wire's national media list costs $550.

BizBest ActionGuide: Call **(888) 381-WIRE**.

J2 Global Communications
(www.j2.com)

At **J2 Global Communications** you can consolidate all your communications. J2 delivers communication services to individuals and businesses (both big and small) worldwide, including Web-based fax, voice mail and conference calling. jConnect Voice Conferencing offers low-cost conference calling with all the bells and whistles. Other features include e-mail, broadcast faxing and Web-initiated conference calling — all with the click of a mouse. Use a j2 number to unify and manage your communications — receive voice mail

★★★	Focus on Small Biz
★★★★	Easy Accessibility
★★★★	Responsiveness
★★★	Vital to Growth
★★★★	Value/Cost
★★	Longevity
Best Feature: Unifies your comm.	
Biggest Hangup: Adapting	

and faxes in your e-mail inbox. No fax machine required. Forward faxes via e-mail and store faxes on your PC. No worries about a confidential fax sitting in a fax tray. jConnect Lite package of services is $4.95 per month (plus usage costs). Premium package is $12.95 per month (plus usage costs).

BizBest ActionGuide: Call **(888) 718-2000**; e-mail: sales@mail.j2.com.

Telephone Doctor
(www.telephonedoctor.com)

★★★	Focus on Small Biz
★★★★	Easy Accessibility
★★★★	Responsiveness
★★★★	Vital to Growth
★★★	Value/Cost
★★★	Longevity
Best Feature: Well organized	
Biggest Hangup: Reality	

Telephone Doctor Customer Service Training, based in St. Louis, is a super place for customer service training info. Find out how you and your employees should *really* be handling the phones. Telephone Doc is known for exceptional training videos. Many customer service training products are specially geared to small biz. Nancy Friedman launched Telephone Doc nearly 20 years ago after receiving scruffy service herself from an insurance agency.

BizBest ActionGuide: Call **(800) 882-9911** and see how *they* answer!

Small Business Owners Ask...
About Calling Plan Comparisons

Dear BizBest: *I'm trying to get the best long distance, wireless and high-speed Internet deals for my business, but I'm confused and befuddled about all the phone company offerings. Help!* — Confused & Befuddled

Telecommunications Research & Action Center
(www.trac.org)

Dear Confused & Befuddled: You're not alone. Finding the best deal among confusing and ever-changing telecom services is tough.

★★★★	Focus on Small Biz
★★★★	Easy Accessibility
★★★	Responsiveness
★★	Vital to Growth
★★★★	Value/Cost
★★★	Longevity

Best Feature: Objective info
Biggest Hangup: Overkill?

Washington, DC-based **Telecommunications Research & Action Center** (TRAC) is a non-profit membership group that offers solid info and advice about selecting plans and saving on long distance. They've been offering excellent telecom plan comparisons and member benefits for 20 years. Publishes *TeleTips Residential and Small Business Long Distance Charts* to help consumers and biz owners make better decisions on their long distance options. Not affiliated with any telephone or other company and does not accept revenues, other than from the sale of its publications, from industry sources. Business membership is $50 for 1 year; $80 for two years. As a member you will receive two residential and two small business issues of Tele-Tips per year.

BizBest ActionGuide: Call **(202) 263-2950**; e-mail trac@trac.org

---

Small Business Owners Ask...
About Remote Conferencing

Dear BizBest: *Our small business delivers proposals to potential clients in distant cities. Usually three of us go, but travel costs are killing us. My partner read about Web and video conferencing and we might want to try that. Can you plug us in?* — Unplugged

Dear Unplugged: No doubt about it, business travel these days is not only expensive, it's becoming a bigger pain in the you-know-what all the time. If you have independent contractors, remote workers, employees, suppliers or customers across the country, phone, video or Web conferencing can be a cost-effective way to get together regularly for on-the-spot decision making. Here's help:

WebEx
(www.webex.com)

WebEx offers a range of multimedia communications, all through a standard Web browser. In particular, the WebEx Meeting Center is great for online meetings with customers, prospects, partners, suppliers and colleagues. All you need is a browser and a phone to interact with customers in real-time. It could help you capitalize on opportunities and boost customer satisfaction.

★★★	Focus on Small Biz
★★★★	Easy Accessibility
★★★	Responsiveness
★★★	Vital to Growth
★★★	Value/Cost
★★	Longevity

Best Feature: Access to tech
Biggest Hangup: Be tech savvy

Using the WebEx Meeting Center, a small business can: 1) present to anyone, anywhere; 2) allow anyone in the meeting to view, annotate and edit any document electronically; 3) share an application on your system or share the entire desktop; 4) use remote control to provide support on the Web and take meeting participants on a Web tour.

BizBest ActionGuide: Call: **(877) 50-WEBEX**; e-mail: info@webex.com.

Section **8**

Human Resources/ Employees

Administaff
(www.administaff.com)

Administaff — a professional employer organization (PEO) — provides a range of staffing services for small to mid-sized businesses, including what you may already know as employee leasing. A key goal is to provide administrative relief for busy business owners who want to spend more time *building* a business and

★★★★	Focus on Small Biz
★★★	Easy Accessibility
★★★★	Responsiveness
★★★	Vital to Growth
★★★	Value/Cost
★★★	Longevity
Best Feature: HRpowerhouse	
Biggest Hangup: Adapting to the PEO concept	

less time with the employer obligations of running that business. Administaff can be the full-service human resources department most small businesses can't afford to have themselves. Services include employment administration, benefits management, government compliance, recruiting and selection, employer liability management, training, performance management and owner support. Administaff has about 40 sales offices in 21 major markets across the country. Administaff can be an excellent option for the small, fast-growing business that can't afford to get bogged down in employer-related expenses and risks while there are sales opportunities awaiting. Administaff, Inc. is a public company with shares trading on the NYSE (symbol ASF).

BizBest ActionGuide: Visit the site or call **(800) 465-3800**. Set up an appointment and get a $50 Office Depot gift card just for listening.

Small Business Owners Ask...
About HR Management

Dear BizBest: *My business is growing and I've assigned someone to be my first human resources (HR) manager. Where can he launch his learning curve?* — Growing

Dear Growing: A new site, **HRpowerhouse.com**, has loads of practical (and free) information that can help your HR manager deal with day-to-day responsibilities. The site is fueled by the HR experts at Administaff, a personnel management services firm, and is chock full of helpful information on topics such as payroll, employment law, benefits, workers' comp and more.

Employers of America
(www.employerhelp.org)

★★★	Focus on Small Biz
★★★	Easy Accessibility
★★★	Responsiveness
★★★★	Vital to Growth
★★★★	Value/Cost
★★★★	Longevity
Best Feature: Help lines	
Biggest Hangup: Small group	

Employers of America — a national membership group for employers, managers and supervisors — calls itself "the boss's association." Helps guide and protect biz owners in their role as an employer. Offers a broad range of help in areas such as employee handbooks, writing job descriptions, posters and many excellent publications. Membership ($99/year) includes *Smart Workplace Practices* newsletter and access to HELPlines. Free 6-week trial membership.

BizBest ActionGuide: HQ: Mason City, IA. Call **(800) 728-3187** or **(641) 424-3187**; e-mail employer@employerhelp.org.

Small Business Owners Ask...
About Virtual Assistants

Dear BizBest: *My home-based biz is growing and I need an assistant in a really bad way, but I can't quite afford one yet. Are there services that can help biz owners like me get help on an as-needed basis?* — Unassisted

International Virtual Assistants Association
(www.ivaa.org)

★★★	Focus on Small Biz
★★★★	Easy Accessibility
★★★	Responsiveness
★★★★	Vital to Growth
★★★★	Value/Cost
★★★★	Longevity

Best Feature: Certification
Biggest Hangup: "Virtual" work

Dear Unassisted: Sounds like you're a good candidate to tap one of the hottest small biz trends of the last several years — virtual assistants. VAs are independent contractors who provide administrative support or specialized services to biz owners from their own location via the Web, phone or fax. The Los Angeles-based **International Virtual Assistants Association** can help you find a qualified virtual assistant for your project, from among its certified membership. The group's Web site offers several directories that help you find a VA by certification, location or alphabetically. You can also submit an RFP and let potential VAs come to you. The FAQ section offers good tips on how to strike up a successful working relationship with a virtual assistant. IVAA is a non-profit organization dedicated to the professional education and development of the Virtual Assistance profession, and to educating the public on the role and function of the Virtual Assistant. IVAA is the only organization offering the IVAA Certified Virtual Assistant exam.

BizBest ActionGuide: Call **(877) 440-2750**.

Small Business Owners Ask...

About Hiring Interns

Dear BizBest: *Other business owners I know have been hiring college interns for years as a source of good, low-cost temporary or summer help. For the most part, they say it's been great. We plan to contact local colleges about hiring interns, but are there other solutions we should try?* — Seeking Interns

InternshipPrograms.com

Dear Seeking: Internships are indeed an excellent source of low- or even no-cost help for small companies, and a great way for students or recent grads to learn about business. Biz owners can easily set up an account and place *free* internship listings at a Web site called **InternshipPrograms.com**, a service of the online career site **WetFeet.com**. InternshipPrograms,

★★★	Focus on Small Biz
★★★★	Easy Accessibility
★★★	Responsiveness
★★	Vital to Growth
★★★★	Value/Cost
★★	Longevity

Best Feature: Wide reach
Biggest Hangup: Good interns still hard to find.

which calls itself an internship search engine, can help you reach over 250,000 job seekers each month and also lets you search a database of candidate profiles and resumes. This well-run site is one of the largest internship communities on the Web and is a great way to find and screen interns.

BizBest ActionGuide: See the site. Call: **(415) 284-7900**; e-mail: internshipprograms@wetfeet.com. .

Small Business Owners Ask...

About Setting Salaries

Dear BizBest: *I need help deciding pay levels for certain jobs. I don't want to overpay or underpay? Where can I*

---

find pay scale info, preferably for free? — Pay Problem

SalaryExpert
(www.salaryexpert.com)

Dear Pay Problem: A super place to collect pay scale comparisons and information is SalaryExpert.com. It's fast and basic salary reports are free. To find the free reports, first select the Professional Version from the home page. Then click on "Basic Salary Report" under "Additional Salary Information for Employers." Select a job title from a pulldown menu of hundreds (from animal caretakers, to bakers, to Web designers and yard engineers). Select a city or enter a Zip Code, hit "Get Report" and you'll receive average salary details for this type of job in your area. The site may also ask for additional details, such as level of skills required.

★★	Focus on Small Biz
★★★★★	Easy Accessibility
★★★	Responsiveness
★★	Vital to Growth
★★★★	Value/Cost
★★★	Longevity

Best Feature: Basic info free
Biggest Hangup: Charges for more detailed info

Reports factor in salary info as well as benefits and cost-of-living. SalaryExpert also offers a range of other, more detailed reports that you can pay for. The Salary Advice section has tips on negotiating salaries.

BizBest ActionGuide: One of the most comprehensive, yet free, salary info resources on the Web. HQ: Vancouver, WA. Call: **(877) 799-3427.**

Section **9**

Government

★★	Focus on Small Biz
★★★	Easy Accessibility
★★	Responsiveness
★★★	Vital to Growth
★★★	Value/Cost
★★	Longevity

Best Feature: One-stop gateway
Biggest Hangup: Navigation

Business.gov

This U.S. Small Business Administration-sponsored site is a one-stop link to all the info and services the federal government provides for business. If you need something — anything — from the Feds that involves business, this single site is your doorway to get there. Categories include: Business Development, Buying and Selling, Financial Assistance, Taxes, Laws & Regulations, International Trade and Workplace Issues. *A handy shortcut to find what you need is to go to the Site Map, which is more like a Table of Contents, organized into subject headings with hotlinks.* Many will simply take you to the appropriate SBA area, while others feed into a variety of Federal entities that deal with small business.

BizBest ActionGuide: Go to **www.business.gov**.

BusinessLaw.gov

One reason small businesses fail is because they don't seek legal help at critical development stages. You can get such help, including info on complying with government laws and regulations, at **BusinessLaw.gov**. This site — launched in 2002 — is specifically

★★★★	Focus on Small Biz
★★★★	Easy Accessibility
★★★	Responsiveness
★★★	Vital to Growth
★★★	Value/Cost
★★	Longevity
Best Feature: State/local links	
Biggest Hangup: Overdose on too much legal stuff	

intended to help small biz owners identify and solve legal and regulatory business questions. It covers all federal agencies and has a section for state and local laws and regulations (select your state from the pull-down menu). Topics range from basics such as choosing a business structure and hiring a lawyer, to specialized issues such as e-commerce and exporting. You can quickly check zoning codes for your local area, or — if you are having problems with a federal regulatory agency — file a complaint with the Office of the National Ombudsman. **BusinessLaw.gov** aims to provide knowledge of basic legal issues so you can identify potential problems early and take action. For a site on legalities of business, run by the government, this is surprisingly good.

BizBest ActionGuide: Helpful sections include: **Plain English Guides** on startup, finance and employees let you use wizards, read mini-tutorials and follow links to gain a basic understanding of the laws that affect a small business. • **Compliance Assistance Directory** helps you locate regulatory help by topic from the agencies that make the rules. • **Enforcement Fairness** helps you know your rights and options. Also has sections on finding/hiring a lawyer, going to court and alternative dispute resolution.

Small Business Owners Ask...
About Government Contracting

Dear BizBest: *I read recently that the Federal government spends billions buying products and services from small businesses every year. How do we get considered for a piece of this action?* — At a Loss

Dear At-A-Loss: Uncle Sam is actually one of the best

small biz customers around — at least in terms of money spent. To get your goods on Sam's shopping list, however, you'll need to learn the ropes of government contracting and get your business listed in the right places. Here are two top resources.

FedBizOpps.gov

Federal Business Opportunities (FBO) is a new Web

★★	Focus on Small Biz
★★★	Easy Accessibility
★★★	Responsiveness
★★★	Vital to Growth
★★★★	Value/Cost
★★	Longevity

Best Feature: Broad listings
Biggest Hangup: Not very small biz friendly

site that serves as a single gateway to all government contracting opportunities valued at over $25,000. Although FedBizOpps isn't especially small biz friendly, it can link you to contracting opportunities at all federal agencies. Try reading the FBO User's Manual first, available on the Web site. To find it, click the "Vendors" button and then on "FBO Vendors Guide." You can download it to your desktop and read at your leisure.

BizBest ActionGuide: If you have any problems using the system, e-mail support@gsa.gov or call the FedBizOpps help line at **(877) 472-3779.**

PRO-Net
(www.pro-net.sba.gov)

PRO-Net — the Procurement Marketing and Access Network — is a government contracting network specifically for small business run by the U.S. Small Business Administration (SBA). List your business here and buyers will find *you*. This is a "self-certifying" database, which means each business is responsible for the accuracy of its own information. Potential buyers of your goods and services will check you out, but there is no policing mecha-

★★★★★	Focus on Small Biz
★★★★	Easy Accessibility
★★★	Responsiveness
★★★	Vital to Growth
★★★	Value/Cost
★★★	Longevity

Best Feature: Easy to list
Biggest Hangup: Self-regulated

nism. Federal, state and even private sector shoppers check the PRO-Net database of nearly 200,000 small businesses to find products and services they need. It's open to all small firms. The service is free to government agencies and private companies seeking small biz contractors, subcontractors or partners. Businesses profiled on the system can be searched by codes, key words, location, quality certifications, business type, ownership and other factors. Once listed, you are responsible for keeping your information current. Nice feature: You can link your Web site to your PRO-Net profile.

BizBest ActionGuide: Visit the site for all the details.

U.S. Patent and Trademark Office
(www.uspto.gov)

★★★	Focus on Small Biz
★★★★	Easy Accessibility
★★★	Responsiveness
★★★★	Vital to Growth
★★★★	Value/Cost
★★★★★	Longevity

Best Feature: Online search
Biggest Hangup: You still need a lawyer to do it right.

Each year, millions of entrepreneurs seek sources to answer their questions about patents and trademarks. Oddly enough, the best place to find answers is right from the horse's mouth: The **U.S. Patent and Trademark Office** (USPTO) itself. Although dozens of private sites offer information on obtaining patents and trademarks, none can match what's available at the PTO Web site. You'll find everything you need, from basic info on types of patents and trademarks, to tips on conducting a search for registered patents and trademarks, those pending, and those that have been rejected or abandoned. To search trademarks, for example, select TRADEMARKS from the main page, then click on SEARCH TRADEMARKS. Enter your search terms and you're there. You can even apply for a patent or trademark online, although BizBest recommends using the services of a qualified lawyer to make sure you successfully navigate this tricky process. A terrific "Frequently Asked Questions" section covers anything you can think of. Site also has a list of approved patent and trademark attorneys.

BizBest ActionGuide: Call the USPTO at **(800) 786-9199** or **(703) 308-4357**. Press 1 for general patent or trademark info. E-mail: usptoinfo@uspto.gov or for specific trademark questions, e-mail: TrademarkAssistanceCenter@uspto.gov

U.S. Small Business Administration
(www.sba.gov)

★★★★★ Focus on Small Biz
★★★★ Easy Accessibility
★★★★ Responsiveness
★★★★ Vital to Growth
★★★★ Value/Cost
★★★★★ Longevity
Best Feature: Answer desk
Biggest Hangup: Self promotion

The **SBA** — which turned 50 in 2003 — is Uncle Sam's main mouthpiece for dealing with small biz. The Web site is massive and filled with goodies — if you know where to look. The **SBA Answer Desk**, at 800-U-ASK-SBA (**800-827-5722**), is the national toll-free telephone service providing info to the public on small business problems and concerns. *This is the place to call for general info about SBA programs, and for routing or referrals to all its programs, services and offices.* The Answer Desk gets a huge volume of calls and e-mails, so you might not get an immediate response, although *BizBest's* calls to this service have generally been answered quickly. A reply to your e-mail (**answerdesk@sba.gov**) can take up to five working days. Hours are 9-5 (Eastern). A makeover of the SBA Web site in 2003 made the home page more visually appealing, and easier to navigate, although once you drill deeper, that tends to disappear. Your five main choices are: Starting, Financing, Managing, Business Opportunities and Disaster Recovery.

STARTING: Includes dozens of articles on startup topics, from finding a niche and protecting your ideas, to writing a business plan, finding capital, tax matters and many others. Offers detailed information on the basics of financing a new business, marketing, hiring employees, licenses, permits and training. A "Special Interest Topics" section includes information for women entrepreneurs, veterans, Native Americans, minorities and young entrepreneurs. Download the SBA's free *Small Business Startup Guide* from this section.

FINANCING: Learn all about raising capital for a business, including finance basics, estimating costs, equity financing, small business lenders and the SBA's role. The section on understanding financial statements is a good introduction and nice refresher for current business owners. (See our summary of key SBA financing programs, below.)

MANAGING: Articles in this section cover planning, management skills and leadership, managing employees, marketing ideas, financial controls and getting on the Web.

BUSINESS OPPORTUNITIES: This section offers detailed information on selling goods and services to the government, including the basics of how the government buys, understanding the rules of government contracting, how to find contracting opportunities (including the SBA matchmaking program), preparing a bid and obtaining assistance from the SBA.

DISASTER RECOVERY: All the resources you need to seek disaster recovery assistance for a small business are here, plus tips on being prepared.

Small Business Owners Ask...
About SBA Loans

Dear BizBest: *I want to find out if my business can qualify for a U.S. Small Business Administration (SBA) loan. My local bank wasn't much help. And the last time I tried the SBA Web site, it was like navigating a carnival fun house. After 20 minutes, I gave up. What are my best options?* — Seeking SBA Loan

Dear Seeking: First recognize that the SBA does not actually make loans itself. It only guarantees loans so that a bank will be more willing to give you the money. Major players such as Bank of America and Wells Fargo are leading SBA lenders, but many smaller banks participate, too. Once you apply, the bank decides if it will make the loan internally or if your application has a weakness that will require an SBA guarantee. There are many types of SBA-backed loans. The one that's right for you depends on the type of business you have and your plans for the money. The SBA itself has the best info and, happily, their newly redesigned Web site is much easier to navigate. Start in the financing section (**www.sba.gov/financing**) or call the SBA Answer Desk at **(800) 827-5722**.

Here are some key SBA financing programs and direct links to their Web pages:

■ The **7(a) Loan Guarantee Program** is the SBA's main small business financing category. It helps secure loans for small businesses that are unable to find financing on reasonable terms through conventional lending channels and will guarantee up to $1 million. Go to **www.sba.gov/financing/sbaloan/7a.html** for complete details on loan terms, application procedures and what the SBA looks for in an applicant.

■ The **LowDoc Program** (for "low documentation") streamlines the process of applying for loans of up to $150,000, with decisions made in less than two days. Once you meet a lender's requirements for credit, the lender may request LowDoc processing from the SBA. It's a two-step process: 1) The borrower completes the front of the SBA's one-page application, and the lender completes the back. 2) The lender submits a complete application to the SBA and receives an answer within 36 hours. A similar program called SBA Express handles loans of up to $250,000. Read LowDoc details at **www.sba.gov/financing/lendinvest/lowdoc.html**. You'll find SBA Express information at: **www.sba.gov/financing/lendinvest/sbaexpress.html**

■ The **SBA CAPLines Loan Program** is the umbrella under which the SBA helps small businesses meet their needs for short-term and seasonal cash with a revolving line of credit. There are five short-term working-capital loan programs under CAPLines, including programs for builders and contractors. For details, go to **www.sba.gov/financing/loanprog/caplines.html**.

■ The **Prequalification Loan Program** targets women, minority, disabled and veteran-owned businesses. Through the program, an intermediary will help you develop a viable small business loan application package and secure a small business loan of up to $250,000. Go to: **www.sba.gov/financing/sbaloan/prequalification.htm**.

■ The **504 Certified Development Company** (CDC) program helps growing businesses obtain financing for major fixed assets, such as real estate and machinery. The non-profit CDCs work with the SBA and private sector lenders to come up with the money. There are about 290 CDCs nationwide. The **National Association of Development Companies** (NADCO; Web site: **www.nadco.org**) has helpful information on this program and a directory of CDCs. Call **(703) 748-2575**.

■ The SBA **MicroLoan Program** aims to increase availability of very small loans to business startups. Here, the SBA makes funds available to non-profit intermediaries, who in turn make loans to business owners in amounts from $100 to $35,000 (average $10,500). The intermediary processes applications. The maximum term for a microloan is six years. Other loan terms vary according to the size of the loan, the planned use of funds, the requirements of the intermediary lender and the needs of the small business. Completed applications usually are processed in less than a week. *BizBest ActionGuide*: Visit **www.sba.gov/financing/sbaloan/microloans.html** or for a state-by-state list of Microloan lender participants, go to **www.sba.gov/financing/microparticipants.html**.

VETbiz
(www.vetbiz.gov)

VETbiz is the Federal government's one-stop Web portal for veteran business owners. This is also known as the **Department of Veterans Affairs, Center for Veterans Enterprise**. **VETbiz** is a resource for veterans who own or want to start a business. It offers info about loans, startup, business management programs, online training and procurement opportunities. This is basically a clearinghouse for information about government small biz programs from a vet's perspective.

★★★★★ Focus on Small Biz
★★★★ Easy Accessibility
★★★ Responsiveness
★★★★ Vital to Growth
★★★★ Value/Cost
★★★ Longevity
Best Feature: Vet perspective
Biggest Hangup: Just a portal

BizBest ActionGuide: Call (202) 254-0233 or **(866) 584-2344**; fax: (202) 254-0238; e-mail: vacve@mail.va.gov.

Import/Export

Alibaba International
(www.alibaba.com)

If your biz is looking beyond U.S. borders to buy or sell products and services, this is a place to visit. Alibaba is among the world's biggest centers for global trade and a top provider of online marketing services to small importers and exporters. Alibaba.com is a major destination for buyers and sellers to find trade opportunities and promote their businesses online. Its Web sites have over a million registered members from 200 countries. You can browse company info and trade leads by 27 industry and 700 product categories. Members post, view and respond to buy, sell and partnership offers. Each day Alibaba.com members post over 2,500 new buy/sell offers. Each offer is screened to insure it meets a clear and consistent format. Members can receive lead updates via e-mail with Alibaba.com's Trade Alert service. Of special interest: The **Business Center** — A one-stop shop for shipping info, credit reports, country reports and

★★★	Focus on Small Biz
★★★★	Easy Accessibility
★★★	Responsiveness
★★★	Vital to Growth
★★★★	Value/Cost
★★★	Longevity

Best Features: Marketing services and trade leads
Biggest Hangup Size of Web site is a bit daunting

pricing; and **TrustPass** — An interactive trust profile designed to help business people win trust, know their partners and display their credibility online. Basic membership is free.

BizBest ActionGuide: HQ is in Hong Kong with a U.S. office in Newark, CA. Call: **(510) 438-7980**; fax: (510) 438-7981.

Small Business Owners Ask...

About Selling Overseas

Dear BizBest: *My partner thinks we should try to sell our products outside the U.S. and that exporting isn't a big deal. But I'm skeptical. Where can we find balanced advice and information about getting into the exporting game?* — Skeptical

Dear Skeptical: Your partner may be right. Selling overseas is one of the fastest growing trends in American small business. But you are also right to approach with caution. Issues such as shipping, collections and customer service get sticky. Fortunately, there's a rich bounty of help for small biz owners. Here are two top resources:

Export.gov

Export.gov is a gateway to all export-related help offered by the federal government. Need info on exporting basics? It's here. How about trade leads, free export counseling or help with shipping and finance? You'll find it all at Export.gov, an excellent first step toward selling overseas. *The home page is clean and well organized.*

★★★★★	Focus on Small Biz
★★★★★	Easy Accessibility
★★★★	Responsiveness
★★	Vital to Growth
★★★★★	Value/Cost
★★★★	Longevity

Best Features: Well-organized site, with A to Z help for exporting and even individual counseling

Main headings include: 1) Export Basics; 2) Market Research; 3) Partners & Trade Leads; 4) Pricing, Quotes & Negotiations; 5) Shipping & Documentation; 6) Finance; 7) Trade Shows & Events; 8) Counseling;

and 9) Help with Trade Problems. This service conducts over 100,000 counseling sessions with U.S. businesses each year to help them find and close overseas deals. Check out the free online edition of *Export America Magazine* for articles and news on export opportunities.

BizBest ActionGuide: For personalized service call the toll-free help line: **(800) USA-TRADE**.

International Trade Import-Export Portal
(www.fita.org)

★★★	Focus on Small Biz
★★★★	Easy Accessibility
★★★★	Responsiveness
★★	Vital to Growth
★★★★★	Value/Cost
★★★	Longevity

Best Feature: Complete menu of products, services & info
Biggest Hangup: No particular emphasis on small business

The **International Trade/Import-Export Portal**, a Web site run by the Reston, VA-based **Federation of International Trade Associations (FITA)**, is an information-rich service with much to offer small business owners looking to buy or sell outside the U.S. *If you could use only one Web site to establish and grow international sales, this would be it.* Among other things, it offers a global trade shop with goods and services you'll need. Departments include: Trade Leads, Market Research, Buy/Sell Exchange and Global Payment Services. Helpful directories listing Export Management Companies and country- or industry-specific resources are some of the best available. Most info is free. There's an amazing database of international trade resources and a huge Calendar of Trade Shows.

BizBest ActionGuide: Call **(800) 969-3482** or **(703) 620-1588**; e-mail: info@fita.org.

Section **11**

Special Sectors

(Disabled • Women • Minorities • Family • Youth)

American Woman's Economic Development Corporation
(www.awed.org)

The **American Woman's Economic Development Corp.** (AWED) is a not-for-profit group that's been helping women start and grow their own businesses since 1976. It's one of America's premier national membership organizations ($29 to $55/year) supporting women biz owners. Based in New York City, with offices in S. Calif., Conn. and Washington, DC, AWED has served over 100,000 women with training, counseling, seminars and networking. The group's goal is to increase the start-up and survival rates of women-owned small businesses. The Web site is attractively-designed and easy to navi-

★★★★★	Focus on Small Biz
★★	Easy Accessibility
★★★★	Responsiveness
★★★★	Vital to Growth
★★★★	Value/Cost
★★★★★	Longevity

Best Feature: Startup advice
Biggest Hangup: Most value for those in New York area

gate. Offers several entrepreneurship training programs, including an ambitious schedule of workshops and seminars held in the New York area for a modest fee. Hour-long business counseling sessions ($29) are also available on dozens of specialized topics, from accounting and advertising, to zoning. AWED will match you with an appropriate expert. For something more intensive, AWED also has a coaching program offering six training sessions over two months for $400. The First Steps program, which you can do online, is meant to help you decide if entrepreneurship is really for you. Check out the AWED online newsletter *InBusiness* for the latest organizational news. In short, AWED has a great deal to offer.

BizBest ActionGuide: HQ: New York City; Call: **(917) 368-6100**; fax: (212) 986-7114; e-mail: info@awed.org.

Family Firm Institute
(www.ffi.org)

The **Family Firm Institute** (FFI) can be an excellent resource if you run a family-owned business. The Institute has a database of family business consultants and speakers, runs conferences and can help you locate a university-based family biz program. (The university-based family business programs can be an excellent resource!) FFI is a professional organization dedicated to helping family firms by increasing the skills and knowledge of family business advisors, educators, researchers and consultants. Members include

★★★	Focus on Small Biz
★★★	Easy Accessibility
★★★★	Responsiveness
★★★★	Vital to Growth
★★★★★	Value/Cost
★★★★★	Longevity
Best Feature: Expert referrals	
Biggest Hangup: For professionals who serve family biz	

lawyers, business therapists, accountants, insurance professionals, educators and other family businesses specialists, as well as family business owners. Membership for a family business is $580/year. Also acts as a clearinghouse for info on the latest trends and developments in family business.

BizBest ActionGuide: Call **(617) 482-3049**; e-mail ffi@ffi.org.

Small Business Owners Ask...

About Help for Young Entrepreneurs

Dear BizBest: *I started a part-time business two years ago as a college sophomore. Now I'm about to graduate, jobs are scarce, and running my own business appeals to me. Where can young entrepreneurs get "connected?"* — Eager Student

Dear Eager: New grads who become budding biz owners are swelling the entrepreneurship ranks. And many organizations — some old, some new — cater specifically to youth interested in business ownership. Here's our #1 choice:

Junior Achievement
(www.ja.org)

Junior Achievement (JA), based in Colorado Springs, CO, is a terrific national entrepreneurship program for youth that's been around for decades (*BizBest* founder Dan Kehrer is a JA alum). At the JA Web site, first find the Student Center, then click Entrepreneur Center to find advice on choosing a business, a business startup kit, a student Entrepreneur of the Year contest, business simulations and loads of youth-centered biz resources. JA also hosts live, online mentor discussions where students worldwide can log in and pose business-related questions to a panel of successful young entrepreneurs. You can't go wrong with this premier educational organization.

★★★★★	Focus on Small Biz
★★★★	Easy Accessibility
★★★★	Responsiveness
★★★★	Vital to Growth
★★★★★	Value/Cost
★★★★★	Longevity

Best Feature: Knows how to talk entrepreneurship to youth

BizBest ActionGuide: Visit **www.ja.org** to find the Student Center or call **(800) THE-NEW-JA** to locate a school-based JA program in your area.

Minority Business Development Agency
(www.mbda.gov)

The **Minority Business Development Agency** (under the U.S. Dept. of Commerce), and its nationwide network of **Minority Business Development Centers**, provides business development information and services to minority entrepreneurs. MBDA is the only federal agency created solely to foster the formation, growth and expansion of minority-owned businesses. Four key sections: 1) Access to Markets, 2) Access to Capital, 3) Management & Technical Assistance, and 4) Education and Training can plug you into corporate and government markets, match you with financing, help you get going with e-commerce and much more. There are five MBDA regional offices (Atlanta, Chicago, Dallas, New York, San Francisco) and four district offices (Miami, Boston, Philadelphia, Los Angeles) where staff members oversee assistance services in multi-state regions. The **RESOURCE LOCATOR**, at the Web site, is one particularly helpful tool for locating local minority business resources. Click on the name under Tools and Services. Enter your city, hit search, and you will be presented with a list of resources in your area. MBDA also has a hand in local business opportunity fairs that sometimes draw thousands.

★★★★	Focus on Small Biz
★★★	Easy Accessibility
★★★	Responsiveness
★★★	Vital to Growth
★★★★	Value/Cost
★★★	Longevity
Best Feature: Regional centers	
Biggest Hangup: Web site could be much better	

BizBest ActionGuide: Best way in is through a regional office or Minority Business Development Center in your area. To locate one, call **(888) 324-1551**; e-mail help@mbda.gov.

Multicultural Marketing Resources, Inc.
(www.inforesources.com)

Multicultural Marketing Resources, Inc. (MMR) is a New York-based marketing company that provides multicultural and diversity news and leading experts in multicultural marketing. MMR publishes the bi-monthly newsletter *Multicultural Marketing News, The Source Book of Multicultural Experts* and the online newsletter *MMR e-News*. MMR also

★★	Focus on Small Biz
★★	Easy Accessibility
★★★	Responsiveness
★★★	Vital to Growth
★★★★	Value/Cost
★★★	Longevity
Best Feature: Access to experts	
Biggest Hangup: NYC limiting	

provides helpful info on how businesses can reach diverse markets. Lisa Skrilof, president, really knows her stuff. _The Source Book of Multicultural Experts_, which sells for $59.95, is an excellent resource for locating multicultural marketing expertise. There's also a free online version featuring "selected" experts from the sourcebook. You'll find it at the Web site. MMR's Reference Library/Knowledge Center is a resource for both new and experienced marketers whose companies target, or help others target, the Hispanic, Asian American, African American, women, gay/lesbian and other markets. The library has basic demographic info on each market, including reports, studies and directories.

BizBest ActionGuide: Visit the site or call **(212) 242-3351**.

Office of Women's Business Ownership
(www.onlineWBC.com)

The SBA's **Office of Women's Business Ownership** promotes the growth of women-owned businesses by providing training and technical assistance, access to credit and capital, federal contracts and trade opportunities. There is a Women's Business Ownership Representative in every SBA district office, a nationwide network of mentoring roundtables, Women's Business Centers in nearly every state, women-owned venture capital companies and the **Online Women's Business Center** (**www.onlinewbc.gov**). All are excellent resources, backed by solid expertise and funding, offering services for free or very low cost. Help is available for every stage of developing and expanding a business. _Highlights_:

- The **Women's Network for Entrepreneurial Training** (WNET) matches successful entrepreneurial women (mentors) with women biz owners whose companies are ready to grow (protégés). WNET works through roundtables, where participants meet to receive practical support and guidance from mentors in an informal, ongoing relationship. WNET offers mentoring at more than 160 roundtable groups nationwide. Click MENTOR ROUNDTABLES at onlineWBC.gov.

- The SBA's nationwide network of more than 90 **Women's Business Centers** (WBCs) provides a wide range of services to women entrepre-

★★★★★	Focus on Small Biz
★★★★	Easy Accessibility
★★★★	Responsiveness
★★★★	Vital to Growth
★★★★★	Value/Cost
★★★★	Longevity

Best Feature: Gung ho effort
Biggest Hangup: Keeping it all going, and fresh

neurs. Each center offers training in finance, management, marketing, procurement and the Internet. All provide individual business counseling and access to the SBA's programs and services; some are also intermediaries for the SBA's MicroLoan and Loan Prequalification programs. Many offer counseling in two or more languages. Click on "Women's Business Centers" at **www.onlineWBC.gov.**

BizBest ActionGuide: Call **(202) 205-6673** or **800-8-ASK-SBA**; e-mail: owbo@sba.gov.

Small Business and Self-Employment Service
(www.jan.wvu.edu/SBSES)

★★★★★	Focus on Small Biz
★★★★★	Easy Accessibility
★★★	Responsiveness
★★	Vital to Growth
★★★★	Value/Cost
★★★★	Longevity

Best Feature: Resource list
Biggest Hangup: Could be more specific to disabled

The **Office of Disability Employment Policy** of the U.S. Department of Labor has a marvelous (if rather obscure) unit called the **Small Business and Self-Employment Service** (SBSES). Its main purpose is to provide *free information, counseling and referrals about self employment and small business ownership opportunities for people with disabilities.* The Web site has lists and links to all kinds of national, state and local small biz development programs and organizations that are extensive and easily available to anyone. *BizBest* has researched hundreds of Web sites that list local, state and regional resources targeting small business and this is one of the best we have found.

BizBest ActionGuide: SBSES is operated in partnership with the **International Center for Disability Information** at West Virginia University and is staffed by DOL's Job Accommodation Network, operating at WVU. Call: **(800) 526-7234** V/TTY; fax: (304) 293-5407; e-mail: kcording@wvu.edu.

Section **12**

Troubleshooting

Small Business Owners Ask...
About Resolving Business Disputes

Dear BizBest: *A former partner and I have an ongoing business dispute we can't seem to resolve. Neither of us can afford to get bogged down in a lawsuit. Where can we get help?* — In Dispute

Dear In Dispute: Look into something called "alternative dispute resolution" or ADR. It's user-friendly, inexpensive and helps resolve thousands of business disputes yearly. Here are two top ADR resources for small business.

American Arbitration Assn.
(www.adr.org)

The **American Arbitration Association** (AAA), based in New York, is an excellent not-for-profit organization that offers alternative dispute resolution (ADR) services, help- ing resolve over 200,000 cases yearly. AAA provides a forum for hearing disputes via 34 offices nationwide,

★★	Focus on Small Biz
★★★★	Easy Accessibility
★★★★	Responsiveness
★★★	Vital to Growth
★★★★★	Value/Cost
★★★★	Longevity

Best Feature: Choices of ADR options and help
Biggest Hangup: Learning curve

using broadly accepted rules and a roster of some 8,000 impartial experts to help resolve cases. Most disputes use mediation and arbitration, but even less formal methods called *fact-finding*, *mini-trial* and *partnering* are being used more by small firms. AAA has excellent ADR publications, plus downloadable ADR forms that can help you head off disputes in the future. Click on *ADR Guides* at the AAA home page. There's also a section on Internet domain name disputes.

BizBest ActionGuide: Visit the Web site at **www.adr.org**; call **(800) 778-7879** or (212) 716-5800.

Better Business Bureau
(www.dr.bbb.org)

The **Better Business Bureau** (BBB) offers help resolving business disputes with common sense alternatives to expensive legal actions. Programs are run through local BBBs, under the direction of the group's national umbrella organization, the Arlington, VA-based **Council of Better Business Bureaus**. BBBs offer several levels of help, from informal advice to structured media-

★★★★★	Focus on Small Biz
★★★★	Easy Accessibility
★★★★	Responsiveness
★★	Vital to Growth
★★★★	Value/Cost
★★★★★	Longevity

Best Feature: Range of help
Biggest Hangup: Need to work with local BBB offices

tion and arbitration. The BBB's Dispute Resolution Division Web site at **www.dr.bbb.org** explains how it works. A program called **BBB Care** helps small businesses and their customers quickly address disputes at low cost without attorneys. More than 100 BBB offices nationwide offer the program. Bureau staff will work with you and your customer to help resolve the dispute.

BizBest ActionGuide: Main BBB page: **www.bbb.org**. Find BBBs at **http://lookup.bbb.org**. Dispute resolution page is **www.dr.bbb.org**; Call **(703) 276-0100**; e-mail: contactdr@cbbb.bbb.org

★★★	Focus on Small Biz
★★★★	Easy Accessibility
★★★	Responsiveness
★★★	Vital to Growth
★★★★	Value/Cost
★★★	Longevity

Best Feature: Security software
Biggest Hangup: Under new ownership

McAfee Security
(us.mcafee.com)

McAfee Security delivers world-class software and service solutions that help small businesses secure and protect their computers and also make their technology work better. McAfee's well-regarded anti-virus, security, encryption and desktop optimization products includes *VirusScan, SpamKiller, Personal FireWall, EasyRecovery* and *QuickClean*. Prices for most products range from $35 to $99. In addition to retail "boxed" security products, McAfee also offers security services by subscription via the Web. **McAfee** is a unit of Santa Clara, CA-based Network Associates, Inc.

BizBest ActionGuide: Visit the Web site for details. The small business sales/support line **(888) 847-8766** is frequently busy. Also try **(801) 772-1891**.

Small Business Owners Ask...
About Testing Web Connection Speed

Dear BizBest: *Slow Web connections were frustrating my business so I switched to a different, high-speed service. It costs more but doesn't seem much better. How I can check?* — Slow on the Web

Dear Slow: McAfee, a maker of computer security devices and software, offers a really cool — and FREE — service that will test your Web connection speed in just a minute or two online. McAfee's **Internet Connection Speedometer**, which you'll find at **promos.mcafee.com/speedometer**, tells you how fast or slow your Web connection is, regardless of the technology you are using, be it dial-up, ISDN, cable modem or DSL. Just go to the site and click Test Now.

Small Business Owners Ask...
About Improving Workplace Safety

Dear BizBest: *A couple of on-the-job accidents have sent insurance rates soaring for another small business owner I know. Maybe its time I got more serious about safety at my own business. Who can help? —* Thinking Safety

Dear Thinking Safety: Accidents can hurt your business in many ways, including lost productivity as well as government fines and possible legal troubles. Here's a terrific resource that can deliver the safety solutions your small business needs.

National Safety Council
(www.nsc.org)

★★★	Focus on Small Biz
★★★★★	Easy Accessibility
★★★★★	Responsiveness
★★★	Vital to Growth
★★★★★	Value/Cost
★★★★★	Longevity

Best Features: Safety training materials and online safety awareness resources.

The **National Safety Council** (NSC), based in Itasca, IL, is an excellent source of workplace safety advice and info. This non-profit operates under a federal charter and is one of the nation's leading safety resources. NSC offers posters and banners, safety publications, software, training programs, videos and more. The "Workplace" section of the Web site has helpful information for small business in areas such as repetitive motion injuries, emergency care, ergonomics and OSHA compliance. NSC offers an emergency preparedness package and info on proper use and handling of chemicals. If you have employees who drive as part of your business, the safe driving materials can be especially helpful. Consulting services are also available. Annual membership of $215-$300 gets you discounts and additional services.

BizBest ActionGuide: Call: **(800) 621-7619**; **(630) 285-1121**; e-mail: info@nsc.org or visit the Web site.

Symantec
(smallbiz.symantec.com)

Norton AntiVirus from **Symantec** ranks among the world's most trusted anti-virus software. Repairs common virus infections automatically, without interrupting your work. Scans and cleans both incoming and outgoing e-mail and defends against script-based viruses, even between virus definition updates. **Norton Personal Firewall** is an easy-to-use

★★★	Focus on Small Biz
★★★★	Easy Accessibility
★★★★	Responsiveness
★★★★	Vital to Growth
★★★★	Value/Cost
★★★	Longevity

Best Feature: Leader in anti-virus solutions
Biggest Hangup: Not always focused on small business

program that keeps hackers out, and your data in. Helps protect confidential data in e-mail, *Microsoft Office* attachments, Web sites and instant messages. Symantec offers both AntiVirus and Personal Firewall as a bundle for $79 and also has a line of related products to provide Internet security and help solve common computer problems.

BizBest ActionGuide: The Small Business Center at the Web site offers helpful computer security tips and a free newsletter. For information on enterprise (multi-user) solutions call **(800) 721-3934**; for consumer products call **(800) 441-7234**.

Website Pros
(www.websitepros.com)

★★★★★	Focus on Small Biz
★★★★	Easy Accessibility
★★★★	Responsiveness
★★★	Vital to Growth
★★★★	Value/Cost
★★	Longevity

Best Feature: One-on-one attention you get
Biggest Hangup: Good, but may not be the site of your dreams

Many small biz owners run into trouble when they sign up for do-it-yourself Web sites and then discover it still takes time and talent and they'd rather have someone else do the work. Or they want professional design help, but can't afford the prices some designers charge. This is where you can find help.

Website Pros is a small biz Web design specialist with over 400,000 sites to its credit and is a one-stop resource for biz owners looking to build a strong Web presence. Offers do-it-yourself solutions, as well as a *custom* *design service* (where they do it for you) and tailored e-commerce packages to give your online store an edge. Work one-on-one with a professional designer to get the site you want. Then tap the search engine and online advertising features. Website Pros sets itself apart from others in this sector by offering individual attention to each small business owner, both before and after you become a customer. There's a lineup of hosting solutions, custom Web site options and Internet advertising choices to suit every budget. Website Pros provides the site design services — behind the scenes — for other big names in the field, including Yahoo! Store, Register.com, DellHost, Discover Business Services, NFIB and others.

BizBest ActionGuide: Visit the Web site or call **(800) GET-SITE**.

About BizBest's Creator

DANIEL KEHRER, founder and CEO of **BizBest Media Corp.**, is one of America's leading experts on small business solutions and has personally researched tens of thousands of Web sites, companies, organizations, publications and other resources. He is a business information specialist and author with over 25 years experience as a business owner himself in Washington, DC, New York and (currently) Los Angeles. His nationally syndicated **BizBest** newspaper column appears weekly in publications owned by such prestigious publishers as The New York Times Company, Gannett and Copley Newspapers. He has written for numerous major magazines and newspapers, including *The New York Times, Washington Post, Los Angeles Times, Kiplinger's Personal Finance, Reader's Digest, McCall's* and others. Kehrer's award-winning small business publications have reached millions of business owners and entrepreneurs nationwide and he has been a frequent guest on radio and television. His books (**Doing Business Boldly: The Art of Taking Intelligent Risks**; **Save Your Business a Bundle**, and others) and columns have been published in multiple languages worldwide, and he's been honored by the U.S. Small Business Administration as a **Small Business Advocate of the Year**.

The 100 Best: Alphabetical List

About BizBest Media

Serving Small Business Owners & Entrepreneurs

BizBest is the only integrated media company in America dedicated to delivering independently-researched and rated solutions and resources for small businesses across all regions and industries. The *BizBest: Connections for Success* directory, *BizBest* syndicated column, *BizBest 100*, *BizBest.com* Web site and related products meet the expanding information needs of growth-oriented business owners, entrepreneurs, consultants, coaches, advisors and business educators nationwide.

BizBest delivers vital decision-making information in easy-to-access formats and helps business owners build competitive advantage by providing a source of trustworthy and independent information and solutions.

Because *BizBest* accepts no advertising, it has developed a trust and bond with its customers and remains the only such service in America. *BizBest* is the authoritative guide to small business solutions, offering thousands of hand-picked resources across hundreds of subject categories, with expert commentary and exclusive *BizBest* ratings.

BizBest Media Corp. has also partnered with **SCORE** to provide small business owners with free, online content and resources through SCORE's Web site, **www.score.org**. *BizBest's* resource-rich Q&A content is available in the Business Toolbox section of SCORE's site and includes questions from business owners seeking solutions to crucial small business problems. Adjacent to each question is *BizBest's* response and recommendations on the best available resources.

www.bizbest.com • (310) 230-6868 • info@bizbest.com

2,000 Solutions for Every Small Business Need, in the Palm of Your Hand!

Order the complete *BizBest* directory with thousands of resources and solutions hand-picked, analyzed and rated by BizBest Media. *BizBest* is commercial-free — there are no ads or sponsors — so the analysis offered by our team of small business experts is totally independent. *BizBest* is normally $198, but is available through this offer at just $79, a 60% discount! Shipping is FREE. Order today.

60% off plus FREE shipping

Order online: **www.BizBest.com**
Call toll-free **(877) 4-BizBest**